THE UNCOLLECTED POEMS

Peter Handley

Tells stories, classically trained. 'Round here that's bullshit', and so it is permaculturaly.

November twenty twenty One.

Dear Lydia,

It's not the Estate We're in;
it's the state we're in.

Peter.
x.

THE UNCOLLECTED

Cover designed by Bob Prophette

Peter Handley
absurdarts@yahoo.com

Printed in the United States of America

First Printing: 2020

ISBN-9798604781104

THE UNCOLLECTED

Written in the first years of the 21ˢᵗ Century the work does not appear chronologically. A bank manager was sufficiently mistaken to believe a story that was told to him in 1999. The pages have been proofed large enough for a reader not to have to write in the margins. To encourage the dying art of pen and ink.

Some of this work first appeared in – AsiaWrites, Auroville Today, Caravan, Chiminea, DoresetEye, Hydrabad 8, Little Mag and Static.

Mambo Jambo.

As is said
I put my story down here
so that someone may take it up
another day.
That at the end
we begin to reflect back
a perfect beginning
risen in the moment
when the flame goes out.
Blown by a wind-rush
or an echo of a moment
that has not sunk
from the collective pattern
of things,
but is continually
remorselessly
re-tuning itself.

Transmodern.

culture,modernistic materialism,atheism,social engineering,free market
economics,the globe,christianity,communism,new credibility,modernistic
critiques.agnosticism,tribalism,terrorism,ethnic cleansing,euthanasia,
cultural diversity.political correctness,love,objectivity,rational truth,liberty,
racism,sexism,imperialism,homophobia.landscape.syncretism,fashion.
existentialist.liberalist.social configurations,spiritual assumptions.
deconstructing deconstruction.love,the reformation.morality.relativity.absolute.
philosophy,realativism,epistemology,conservatism,fundamentalism.
evangelical,contemporary,confusion,MORALITY.industrial revolution,
revolution,enlightenment.romanticism,marxism,fascism,positivism.
catastrophe, humanism,postmodernism,scientific rationalism,paganism,
babelites,luddites,trophites,socialism,totalitarianism,monolithic sensibility.
communication,LOve,post marxism,Love,architecture,literature,culture and
sub-culture.sexuality,aesthetic,freedom,democracy,theological and non
theological.Logos.manifestation.heritage.counter culture.neo paganism.
neo neoism.millennium,assumption,universal,universality,heirachy.
supernatural,supranatural.natural.LOVe.dialectical,exploitative,information,
society,technology superhighway communication thing.

Desi attitude.

'as a Indian I feel that globalisation is
never ending process and each a every
country should participate in it.
Globalisation should makes you feel like
world is not contents, only enemies and
opportunists but friends and well wishers
also. Globalisation gives you broad state
of mind that will help you
in this professional world.
Everybody should think about peace
and prosperous life. Globalisation doesn't
mean that someone rules you who is
powerful in every manner but you will feel
like you are also part of this world
and you are contributing a small share
ongoing process and lives peacefully.
Globalisation is a very nice idea
subject to nobody can rule you
against your wishes and everyone feels
like they are not from any one country
but belongs to whole world
and contributing their share
live peacefully and prosperously.
Thankyou.'

What you do with What you've Got.

You stay until you're local
making jokes in a tongue become your own
and the money inevitably runs out
though there was never much anyway.
A gypsy now you plead for more
from the throne on the street.

You've lingered a little and spent
your energy on the many and the few
disgarded advice and put platitudes
in their place, not often but enough.

You've given more than you've taken
and you think that's no bad thing
the shirt on your back is still there
though it may need a wash
whilst mourning another half half
a world away, close by you.

You've kept silently mostly and let labels
attach themselves, they know
as they crucify their characters
only they cannot understand without.

You've been regarded by the men
and the women both, the damaged goods
but to get more involved with this?

Those destined to make reparations
on the damage, on the living,
call it transformation, they need it,
call it what you will, standing in front
you're far from here, out of it.

Allegories on the banks of the Ganga.

Dining out on English
delving into words
Talking turkey once or twice
about Kashmiris or the Kurds.
I add a little colloquial
a swear word or some slang
and wait for other languages to concur
that a bang is just a bang.

Mute.

No more words please, last orders at the bah, bah bah
Language has literally arrested faith between faiths
our lifetimes of forgetting, to move forward
between the position that makes hungry dogs bark
or the lame seek solace on the crutchless stop of beggardom.

Where are the archers and infantry, buccaneers, captains of tomorrow
Seers, prophets, idiots and idealists, fools to kinsmen and kings.
A small fight for the final great lost cause, please.
Have we coca-collared on yet to the Priests of the Golden-Bull?

One more word, after we climbed the hill, remember, on the descent
distributing dog-ends like darshan to a smiling socialite saddhu
encamped on the slope, entertaining guests around a small fire
He has seen silence, I can see, in his eyes, beyond,
not for nothing he wants for nothing, nowhere, somewhere still.

Further down amidst the creeching miaow of peacocks,
mayuried into indifference, cavorting with softer cadences
sought by the wise or the wilting, not one drops its' proud plumage
until, somewhere in the Gujurat a knife is twisted in the skin of innocence.

The last word, I notice, written on the Pillars of Hercules in blistered heat
that big fish in little ponds are less active than the smaller ones
and rise for air, that other world, more often than the rest
well water is deep, fish say unaffected by the tides
sweeping through his and her story to put hope an egoless horizon.

Later, I see, the moon casts no shadow on all things less than we are
the laughter of silver white fractals shooting through the finite again
shining light on the cock-crow-of-crackling fires, burning,
upon the hill-top of our concern, sometime, soon, without words.

Either with us or Against us.

It's true, I have been here before, redefining the circle
and editing again, the past, reflections inside history
like a square could never be such without rounded sides.
But listen, listen as you first tried to speak

Equal is as equal does and unity is something together no?
none of us hastened towards the dawn that has not broken yet
so fast. Did they? Yet we know it comes
as sure as the lark the new poisoned bird
we hear sing on the wing above chemical stained trees
on the wing of melancholy of late but true to itself,
sharing with us great secrets of time's tide.

Even listen to the whisper that is gathering ground
in the grass, beneath the soil, in the very white unsunned root
that's never had nor will 'til then see the light that is our day.
It comes, we know it comes, so swift, so fast
we fail to recollect the speed of our own time passing
as if minutes were hours and the days far off.
Like an eon in an hour glass we are trying to parade truth.

Ungalukku Aga – Pour Tous – For You.
In any language.

Simple rhymes and simple words, some images to use
of how and why we choose to live amongst the neighbours we abuse.
I sat in freedoms' chamber once and thought of liberty
and wondered if it's really true that Everyman is free.
From this high spot I cherished so the nature of my living
and contemplated suicide for all that is not giving.
There's little how and less of why and even better never
that we should find those ego-less, the self ordained, too clever.
The carousel grew mighty quick and slowly spat out money
neglecting to ask itself the truth of those who work to bottle honey.
It really has to stop somehow, a correct position re-aligned
most gathered as refugees round villages for the future to re-define
but colluding with past inventions old for psychic safety's sake
is like adding coffin nails to ingredients to bake a babys' birthday cake.
If there's want to show progress, the God inside's without
for I never heard exploitation say it made us more devout.
It's not for whingeing critics sake I scribe a bold reflection
only that inside ourselves we've lacked to check intention.
So as you sit in cosy chat, let's say, around your retired wine
reflect upon the truth there is in living the real life divine.

Thursday and the Supramental. East.

The soul fed irony of life
Predominates the lonely, scattered in the woods
a once barren landscape now fertile with green hope.
We will laugh, should there be, after this
On the two-sided face of tomorrow
lacking the simple symmetry of uncomplex time
the becoming time, beyond our nervous chatter
climbing higher to the pinnacle beyond the existence
above the raggle taggle masses and into the mind.

All but nothing and none sense, nowhere but here.
'The undamned flood of that universal energy'
gave birth to the rise of the truth that will out.
Every dog that had its' day has fallen
chewing on the hippocrisy of its' own hind leg,
Hungry for more.

The Twelve Adherents.

I found sincerity in living
and small humility in love
some gratitude in sharing
the great perseverance from above.
in aspiration I was seeking
the receptivity from the good
and the progress I was making
coursed blue courage through my blood.
Now the goodness I'm promoting
creates generosity in kind
and the equanimity I'm finding
Sustains my disinterested peace of mind.

Wayste Paper.

Walking back from lunch with the Bengali and her daughter,
she, off to a threatened epi-centre of a conflagration after describing
by default, her disdain of the Britishers, through that not said.
In the road, amongst the rubbish of modern village living
that cannot be recycled sold or burnt, a page from a school book
the grease betraying it's use to wrap fast food, samosa, pakora.
Words laying wasted on the red earth of a scorched land
numbered one to fifteen in no order, red and blue ink
handwriting getting to grips with the written form
it goes like this

11. No isn't a bell. Statement
13. is it a book. Yes it is a book
12. Are we boys. Yes we are boys
15. Are we mans. Yes you are mans
14. are we pencils. No they aren't a pencil
1. Am I Poleic. Yes I am Poleic
    2. Is he a doctor. Yes he is a doctor
    3. Is she a fox. No isn't she a fox.
    4. Is it a flow. Yes it is a flow
    5. are we pens. Yes we are pens
    6. Are we homes. Yes we are homes
    7. Are they trees. Yes they are trees
    8. Am I banana. No am not bananas

I read this. Then I re-read this. Then I read again,
In the quiet of the wind that blows through the hut
that is my home, as seven sister birds argue
with a snake in the grass about territory and belonging.

I would like the next instalment, the next lesson
to come fallen in the wasteland to teach me more.
Nothing will come, there is no more.
I must be satisfied with these abstractions.
Are we pens. Yes we are pens.
Is it a flow. Yes it is a flow.

Society Member.

Who at the beginning of their alphabet
could also meet the end ?
Mr. Gupta raging in his obscure mind
at the balance sheet and receipt
the work not done to satisfaction
in the nature of a man with one bullet left
then a smiling invitation to the society t'boot
the way we roll like evaporating oceans
under a hot and luminous sun
'and you won't need to struggle.'
Mr. Gupta can meet the end
He smiled and told me
so.

Serve Yourself and Save.

On the eve of a small but powerful nuclear conflict
we sit and discuss the merits of spiritual massage
and talk of words to delete from dictionairies.
We are cultured, cultivated, refined and artificially prepared.

It's only a game, we say, we play with ourselves
yet even so the list of all that could be
by political coercion is never complete
until the being within us is abated.

Shockwaves and rumblings and the immediate requirement
someone I quote, is to create conditions precluding
the use of such weapons. 'That is to say
not going to war is the first post dictionary condition.'

Hate, crisis, culture, emotion, fear, harsh, solution, logic
are what we began with.
Servant, problem, slavery, brother, no, law, hunger, good
is how we go on.

Play.

The boy knew he did not look well, carrying the sword
thrusting it, side slashes, in and out of the mangoes and papaya.
Two pieces of wood tied at right angles to one another.
Maybe it was not a sword at all, but he practiced it
outside the grocery shop by the quiet village bakery.
There he was, cutting into the whole world
expending his breakfast for the want of a cause.
My three matches and a beedie later
he reflects on the weapon.
Maybe it is just wood, two sticks tied together,
maybe tonight he can carry it across midnight
and into his dreams.

'Ohm Shakti.'
a tea shop next to the City of Dawn.

The view of the city from this gateway village
is a green and pleasant encroaching ghetto
attired in the garb akin to the future now.
This breed of the new conscious, have to pass through
a life led by the ordinary, for we are,
retiring to the urban human apiary
while charters drawn and blessed with love
throw daggers like a lazy dream
at the stonewall of indifference,
sceptics of the acceleration that stands still.
A little progress in nature, not unlike ourselves.

In the regional headquarters of the World Social Forum
A tea shop, Ohm Shakti.
Old men, wise as the night, sit leperless
in the afternoon heat, even beggars have to relent.
Proclamations were made today, to shake the tree
that holds the key, to this we call divine anarchy.
To feel the ground beneath the feet, pulling
from the tree root of eternity, into now.
We sit, debating, imported ideas amongst the minority.

We are taking tea and biscuits
talking about the global condition
in the quiet village as teeth decay from too sweet tea.
Tractors full laden with a shower of pest killer
pass through to cashew groves growing silently
a cash crop for subsistence under a ripening sun.

Conversation turns to travel to and from the north
where climates change they say and children dance
barefoot in the street.
We have proscribed the full meaning
of our latent positions and passed peacefully

around our own contrition.
Until we shun the bleeding cups
that fill and empty to our pregnant pause,
we shall not know, only be the experiment.
This day that has refused to shake our lazy egos.
Casualties of an economic war, and more
the refugees from development.

Opposite, Lakshmi sits floorwise in a Delft doorway
wrapping cotton around jasmine buds, smile full.
Her children play languidly in the heat.
Tension in the tea shop over absentee masters
set adrift yesterday on drunken arrack benders, a reprimand.
He stands his corner with a matchstick in his ear. Leaves.
A warm east wind blows over the tree tops from the sea.
The vegetable seller wipes toothbrush spittle into the pile.
Three mozhums have been wrapped in this short time
on the small blue stool standing as the market place
for fragrance and beauty.

Justice did exist, resting only a while
a small respite from diction
during the discussion about Us and Them.
There seemed little point, as if the lights went out,
as if, in the darkness only a dim light shone through.
The pursuit of it has made grown men lean
on the fat of philosophy.
And now some labouring under famished skies
to take the skeletal framework of the future tense
colliding with that other nervosity, borne of the willing.

The scales are out, hanging from a tripod
to weigh in the cashew crop collectively,
it seems as if the whole village men are out
by a cart to unstuck the tethered hooves of an ox
stretched on it's side, suffering a small loss of liberty.

Gaggling young women clucking between houses
while at the top of the road pastured oxen cry anxiety.
Nothing, much, matters, today, beyond the evening fire.

Towards the end as the heat built
cashew still being drawn to the ground to bleach and dry,
people running to their houses to take stock, make accounts
drawing sides and concluding decisions to stand
on either side of a wall that separated unity from itself.
Some talk of village service nodes where dreamers
could come and interact with real people, from time to time,
pulling science fiction towards science fact.
By now the walls are built and the flimsy headed
beat a retreat to the urbanity of daily living.
Dreamers moved to the field where more tangibility grew.
The diplomatically political renamed themselves
throwing caution to a wind that would not blow.

Unstuck and on the road the laden cart passes
within earshot of the ordered chaos from a tourist's mouth.
The shopkeeper, keeping cool under fire, shares his bemusement
and we laugh together at his disability, casually.
Sun sets and content comes on, walking west, home
against the traffic again, across the grain
all the way, up hill, home
to my little fortress and a dried up moat.

The plough shifts in silence across the northern sky
A slow-motion-celestial-cart-wheel-west.
Dogs barking at nothing but the shadows
will chase their voices around a circle as bright as dawn.
For now, this red earth, sleeps.

New York Conversation.

She's not a little disturbed, as you suggest, I say she's traumatized
in the foment of her little body functions releasing shattered nerves.
A trauma review could be made that would show the root of her condition
coming from the drought of humanity lulless, between the ghost of twin towers.

Sent by sanity's search for self and an errant mother's malignance,
seeing temples still and not temperaments, dollared dust on her mind
I count her as the fourth today in as many hours, to pass by,
Geez-US, we sit in strange secular service nodes, offering mutual addictions.

She has become the self-ordained guru-of-not-giving
in the visceral vernacular, a venomous bitch, if judgement had it's day.
Her present parentalled condition seeks hospitals as the hotel to relax
to build stories of injustice done, solely to her floating wallet and fates' cause,
these are her temples to the source of her mendicant divinity.

Ah, the little pioneer of self searching catastrophe
(to travel with her, she says, is to risk the wrath of a once crossed god)
Where would she be without the recall in rhetoric of incident and accident
to belly up and full disguise her damnated docile life.

I mention her now after listening for quite some time
to escapees and refugees, travellers and the travelled, lost and lingering
those who in polite society might be sedated within at least four walls
or perversely curing the ill at ease, the maladroit, atrophied touring anarchists.

I default on my description a little having held humour upto the light
after all, laughter that does not turn to tears only reveals locked secrets behind smiles.
But for her, I cannot contrive an ending more suitable, than this she knows.
It's no more a wish than to see a cat in a cradle or cows jump over the moon.

Naipaul was only Joking.

Only fine and unexpected friends
share their sugar bowls these days,
having cracked and thrown mine out.

At the print money shop somewhere
in the never never land of the spirit resort
pcople – in their supra-mental
guard spoons like rare lost jewellery.

Across the waters, oceans, skies
a war ravaged cess-pit of a village
raped and stained with the blood of oil.

Offers come to entertain my stay
to grow thinner on the dilemmas
of family, friends, forgotten futures.

Where to be now, a foreigner
in a foreign land or a foreigner
at home in a sun baked skin.

A Portrait.

I am told this morning I am chronically fatigued,
Body tired, mind shut down
I do not think that this is so
Though for sure the body has gained in what it lost.
My source tells me that when the brake is depressed
We only accelerate.
I mumble something about travelling further if we stand still,
having spoken about such things before
may do so again in a dharmic reality
So it takes no energy in the re-telling.
About conversations with the body,
How we learn to speak to ourselves
That we must learn to love love for love's sake.
Each has his motor tuned to its own understanding
For sanity's sake.

Now no words, used up in total for others.
This social therapy calculated as laziness
Though there are those hapless in my absence.
In the tea shop
Along the entrance road next to the barbers' saloon
vegetable stall bakery and general store, people,
Lacking creed or colour traverse the road
To their nirvana.

Mr. Gupta Forgets.

'   *when your neck is being trampled under the tyrants' heal*
       the safest course is to keep on tickiling his feet'. Premchand.

Morning begins with the psychology of dogs
And quickly moves to laboratory talk
After discussing the merits of a tin of sardines
Or the disbenefit of toilet paper in extreme heat
We rambled about a famous poet, how he plays with us.
Not exactly in the barrack room
But somewhere near the stores.

The evening is arranged between discussions
About sons who have some imbalance.
Between teas. After breakfast. Before lunch.
Whole conversations in a foreign tongue
I understand from cadence, inflection, tone
And the sound-of-the-world.
I am the king of the castle of concern.
We are our foreign tongues.

In the bookshop, after words, I search for clarity
In totality, having grown lean on Summer fruits.
I see, Mr Gupta takes his raincoat from beyond surrender
And forgets. At the border the weather closes in.

Time on the Scaffolding.

I have begun telling the watch laden time
plucked righteous from air as hard as nails
Some overbearing excess gives grieving hours
more minutes to this psychics realm.
And well before the hands that turn
False humour into seconds caught
we gayley pass the future on
wishing our own sweet content some way.

The History of Truth.

Truth was the most of many credibles,
More first, more always, than a bat-winged lion,
A fish tailed dog or eagle headed fish,
The least like mortals, doubted by their deaths.

Truth was their model as they strove to build
A world in that ago when being was believing,
of lasting objects to believe in,
Without believing earthenware and legend,
Archway and song, were truthful or untruthful:
The Truth was there already to be true.

This while when then, practical like paper-dishes,
Truth is convertible to kilowatts,
Our last to do by is an anti-model,
Some untruth anyone can give the lie to
a nothing no one need believe is there.

The Line of Control.

the build up on the borders continues
while diplomats come and go to appease.
I've a cartoon stored in the memory
of two opposing sides each barking
across a thin blue line.

Behind the first side, armed to the hilt
is an American soldier, poised in reserve,
gun cocked, scared shitless and fully trained.

Behind the second side, armed to the hilt
(are we still taking sides?)
is an American soldier, poised in reserve,
gun cocked, scared shitless and fully trained.

A soft drinks man passes by, coca-cola, tm,
Behind the sides, fully trained, scared shitless.
He also plays the game of double jeopardy
While foreign embassies are making plans
And calculating the future need.

Grandfather. Armistice day.

Today we remember the dead as we kill
learning nothing from history, family ,the lost
and we laugh into this glass called safety.
What we have won, what we have lost
we should remember them.
The battles we have with ourselves
great invocations are needed to dull
the equivalence of *this* great war.
Deepavali, Ramadan, the bombs keep falling
before my time and after I presume.

Walking the Elephant Home.

I have begun the journey having seen inside matter
carrying the Keeper's stick in my trunk
the brass bells on chains across our backs
alert the coming but have no weight.
We stop ,at intervals and confer grace on neighbours
for a small reward, never for nothing this way home.
Yesterday I walked the same route with it, I remember
We did the same things yesterday, always showing the way
When the way showed us didn't it.

Ranjit suggests the added significance of the colour
white, as surely as the path to it's cage I'm knowing
it has no colour here, does not care for the race,
under the grease paint.
The beat of its natural heart is also shared by mine
and the base pulse of the earth. It's more evident.

Still the wounds will not heal, on the tarmac path
and I notice my feet, unblistered, even after hot coals.
This big grey heart has glimmered freedom in moments
between steps that lead to sleep, tethered, standing,
hay for a bed and wild marigolds around the door.
He will enter willingly having no fear for the night.
I too will sleep in the cage thinking many things.
It's not important for this animal to be
what is expected of him to be in me, for you.

The Keeper shares his secret of being kept with me
he says to be the new Indian one must keep the Indians
out. It's not remonstration and the elephant agrees
knowing the only thing left behind is knowledge forgot
An exchange has occurred of this we trinity are sure
Tomorrow we take the same route to the Temple
and confer blessings on the same as before.

Addiction @ 37k Feet.

Over Istanbul and that black sea, latticed land like fetid lard.
I realise I can smoke, for the first time at this altitude.
Not from the first of the eighth month my attendant tells me
while urging with a train-ed smile, my enjoyment.
And I'm not sure, the flush of oxygen safe from nicotine
coursing through my veins is simply enough and more
to rush me out over the clouds, out over Europe, Egypt perhaps
(though not confirmed) and into India
where other curses that are not mine
take the bait
at ground level.

the end of radio lines.

wayeed	rising	
byoohn	falling	
byeeed	stretching	
vyazeez	longing	
shayee	cursory	
doomee	resigned	
levine	definite	
sadaahm	*praise*	*(writer's inflection)*
quadroon	comma	
mshahhh	full stop.	

breath

fee-lall   new sentence
spit
spit twice
thrice
and repeat, pause
then bless, lilt, tilt and bend
learn by heart and then pray.

Break.

A Religious Learning @ 37.2k Feet.

The landscape is like tiger skin, warped, weft and matted
running botheways, but south, over oppressed like patchwork,
clockwork the captain will say, adjusting his time differential
Only abstract for my lack of understanding of the script
My OBFM* tells me in green that the centre of the world
is two hours away and radiating.
My destination a mere ripple and reverberation
at the edge of the pool a bend in the river
a cloud on a mountain
Another Mecca, Jedda, Hyderabad, Islamabad
New York Rome.

*on board flight monitor

Weighted, Alert, Alive.

The monitor's almost a memory
of landscape, skip over navels,
the chest groin and ankle
of the world, beautiful.
All this geography sitting behind a man's head
flying like a bullet oblivious.

Before the air in a car on a road that has become
a placebo for national health depressants
I explain the nature of it all
and watch how the driver swears
he'd lock me up
if I weren't his brother.
I should make him aware of speed
cameras
but know his SLR will not repeat
on me. Today.

Beneath the Red Sea and Me only conversation.
No competition at last.

Sparkling Ideas.

Hypo-allergenic twist chain
give as good as you get.

Citizen eco-friendly watches
with an international guarantee

Eternal symbol of devotion, save thirty pounds.
highly covetable

Inspired by a noblewoman's jacket of 1610
Shakespeare would have been proud
of his sonnet locked in an engraved silver locket.

Even princesses need to keep things tidy
with this Disney Princess jewellery box.

A minimalist take on the military identity tag
can be yours for a song, singer.

Residual Shopping.

'eliminate the superfluous, emphasise the comfortable,
acknowledge the elegance of the uncomplicated.' Armani.

Exclusive to inflight retail
the King of casual elegance.
Eco-friendly watches run
on natural or electric light
with a manicure friendly deployment clasp.
Imagine that.
Eco-drive perpetual calendar
adjusts itself for leap years until 2100.
Imagine that.

Tough meets trendy design ethos
used by Nasa astronauts, lightest on earth
unhinged Temples make them impact resistant,
the ultimate unisex luxury travel accessory
invaluable for carrying unforeseen purchases.
Platinum plated accents… imagine.
For a smooth running high-spec life.
Imagine that.
for a smooth…
an advanced phonetic spell correction facility
crank the handle to keep a style conscious owner
happy for hours. Imagine.

Thirty random sounds and a distinct personality
watch them interact, big fun for tiny hands –
a new look for the twenty first century.
…or alleged breach of any applicable law
or regulation. Imagine.

Sanctions @ 37.8k Feet.

Scrubbed clean over Cyprus and   Saliki
which sounds and looks   the same
in Arabic, Emirates, at   any rate.
Crop up against Carver   audioed by an in flight Qu'ran.
Notice cribbing from Armitage   see clouds over Yorkshire
Jihad in Bradford   Smack heads in Rome
dream of Suki, Sara,   Sarah and Anne
mull over the garden of eden   before
and the snakes in the bag.
Lon-dones and duck jokes
and dumb Liverpudlians.
Oil refined Landscapes over Tripoli   remind me
to play chess   more often
climb a mountain   talk to my neighbour
open the door, get sucked in,   at this height.
Over the whirlpool of the world.
Talk to angels over the radio   begin to listen to the bug that bites.

Advertisemeant.

Soar to new heights
with skyward new
gold and silver mem - bers
skip across a silken patchwork
and make up yer points t' glory
Is this trade mark copy right ?
Please move over
the sky's falling in.

Listening to a Holy Word for a while @ 37.9k Feet.

After so much singing of this   spoken book
I begin to hear the rhythm,   not the language
remember Mr. Jones telling   me
about that sign languaged   monkey wrote
for extinction, between   themselves
floundering, in a quarry,   at a crossroads
Cuffra, Cairo   Kuwait, Dubai
eleven thousand metres above the din
I'm told the outside temperature   on the Kaffee Fassett ground
supports the poor   subsist and subside
beneath vapour   steam made by the rich
beneath the rich in the air.

Fantasy in fragrance.

For seductresses, beyond paradise
a multi faceted bottle;
distinctive, intimate
addictive.

Reveals the star in every woman of elegance
a flowery heart and modern softness
for a woman true to herself –
a provocation of rose oil
mysterious and enveloping notes.

coal tar.

Masculine allure
sporty aroma, sensual base notes
a nocturnal signature
a hymn to freedom and harmony.

It's all you want to wear;
instant radiance, perennially popular.

Buy any product onboard and get
a pedometer for only ten pounds.

Shopping the World.
Shopped.

Dear Madam,

Firstly I must apologise for men
like straw chaff in a strong wind
blow fickle through the heat.

I send my belated birthday greetings
to your bed ridden body, my late arrival,
sitting penning under your Ho Chi Minh
next to another fossil of my decoration
older than a world, a divine stone imprint.

Now I hear of your release from said bed
to see you soon and rah the Oxbridge with you
I hope, how you think it is there, before the war.
How I am, I see you, in the glory chair
holding reign over this pecked allotment
living history that we all are here.

Then a story over beer about a man
who courted you, sold speed on two wheels
from an imperial nation, offered paintings
to your love some time ago.
The gold on your Deepavali wrists denies
the service boys some bonus
I begin to see how we piss on this
learning from history passing, to see your face
again, behind the pleasant mask.

Le Quatorze Juillet.

(le beourgeoise gentilhomme qui habite une place d'humilite, pondre des personnes qui don't give a tosse)

Here we salute the oppressed and the oppressor. Where else should we be?
Somewhere between diplomacy, dilemna and dichotomy I sit
while around me the invitations fly like diamonds, lost in a gold mine
or lost wills in a sea of wilt a bracelet bandaged as a charm.
Chutney chews the cud with others a farmer sits, surveys the farm.

Too slowly fore me begins the inculcation, family, friends about
ground level and another time children of the gods we march
until we are incomprehensible abstained like voters
in a voidless world.

Not for the first time under an UN mandate can I, do I, hear the voice
of beligerence against the self. The glory bell that keeps the keel straight
against the shore. This violence against us all in a war torn, grief stricken
land of bounty and opportunity eat the bitches is what we've said.

We count saviours and sheep both as victims,
throw glory into a wind named democracy,
while we develop the attitude
that pins the rest of us to the wall.

Two Rue Francios Martin.

Elizabeth comes to clean for the first time
small robust and tamilike, smiling ivory
she'd be first on the president's podium fer blow jobs
in the politicians office, 'but this is india
not somewhere foreign not the bloody raj.'

I throw dog-ends into the divide above the crossroad
Above the tumult my place on someone elses' hill
Staring so far into nature and tradition
the bleeting of politicians and devotees so say,
barely skims the breeze
the surface of this languid air.

Words land like a medic on a battlefield
remember, language like bummers still steal from the dead.
Caught aimless in beggared attitude baking like bread.

Werk.

through such long sufferance and pouring of water
the all seeing Amar sweeps without a word, knowing everything
cleaning like a nervous reaction to our nervosity
she would bark like a bitch, if she thought it were worth it
what's the point she thinks, above it all
there's no addiction here for a longing for honour
only another day in a shanti paradise.

Fatigue.

light falls through lattice on the stairwell
foliage plinths lye empty, monolithic gods
while bags of light strewn in window winds
hang listless by a thread connected.
Holy smoke from this room blows past paintings
yet to be crafted, as broken dreams
fall like salt on a fresh swept pavement.
on the crossroads of tomorrow
where we collect our debt
even landlords will get a mention
for their specialism in this field.

The terror and beauty of plain lives.

It's easier to find sympathetic answers, wisdoms here
Tea and indian masalas never tasted so good.
They're running around for little retail therapy,
salivating.

I'm a mayday monopolist the articulate anarchist
the beourgeoise homme, pukkar gentleperson, as if.
I'm the blaggard, the beatnik, the bugger, the bone
I'm the arsenal and weaponry triggered by home
is where the heart is, sletsleavitathat. The Gall of it.
The gaul you say, this bladderfull and bilbous tension,
fit for a skin no bigger than a nutmeg egg.
Blacker than brown and white as the night, pure as anything
burnt, stretched washed and blessed, I'll take this course
as far as it came.

18.08.01

'truth does not do as much good in the world
as it's counterfeits do evil.' Rochefoucauld, Maxims. 1678.

one small red unpropagated seed
with one jet black spot
holds round time to ransom
at an axis slower than itself.

that it should be so
is remarkable only in that
it is divorced from the tick
and the tock
of some greater seed bank,
latent propogation
next to it, a bigger botany
on a barred window
sill, staring at the sun
waiting for water
hoping for life.

catching the wind behind him
the New Hercules rushes forward
the scent of a previous century lingers
like dawn on a Sunday to a Christian.

we don't progress, he says, we process
repeat ourselves, take time like a thief
and incarnate the second hand
feed it peas and politic
with both hands scolded by sunshine
and rhetoric.

warriors born of Gods from mortals
don't waver in these tides of confusion.
black tea and brown bread sustains
the morning's appetite
and Bacchus helps thin gravy down.

She Will.

In their idleness
before the dawn
Young disciples decipher
the old mans' yawn.

But now, she

She has the lean curiosity of youth
about her, untempered by experience
and her words that fall bestow
her fragile opportunity to the world.
To feel burnt or blessed or both.

Street food eating at Velangani's

the dead lye in pools of flies
on the front of the Tamil Thandi
while meantime, the meanest of the mean
young men pass judgement
on the hard working mother
she is, she will be and still she was.

Proposal.

she sleeps in the doorway
and I love her for an instant
offering marriage she says her name
beautiful, husband gone, never been
could never surmount the obstacle.
Playing thankyou's with toy balls
before sleep, with children, the dream
the beauty surpassing everything.
This my life, my work
the very being given to everyone.
From here, chrysanthemums hang on the wall
like a leper losing his skin
that is all.

Some borrowed time.

Because she lived on the street, in the park,
with her sister and the children, may be mother
maybe not, but because of this
she could not come in.

Because the colour of her sari
or the neatness of it's trim
like a flower out of time in wrong gardens
dead season, dormant like drought
beyond the fringe at the edge, by a river
dieing, but because of this
she could not come in.

Because she haggles for a home and a cooker
for her family and her health in the best way
of the knowledge she possesses for herself
in the sharing of the living and the dieing
in this wealth this way
she could not come in.

Absent for some time now
jostling, jabbing, smiling at the gutter
dreaming of the sky blue in eternity
she wears the ring.
A gold chain lies sleeping in the seed bank
of the windowsill, staring out to sea;
the view the bay and further off beyond .

Some Transparency.

Some people tell me my mind is lost
and to this I can only say of course
after the advice about not giving advice
and not for the first time to myself,
the cigarette butt, but, must be extinguished
on my thigh, the inside bit
(some self immolation for pain)
I advise myself against it.
So love, truly, never dries up.

The next, some Madam Ammar
offers the ultimatum I will not accept
simply the music too loud
or the kids from the street
visit too often and all of this is repitition
and my right course the correct course
grows longer by the day.

I take a vow of silence, abstinence.
Begin again the long trawl
through a dark wood
blind yet very seeing.

Male Ego.

How we laughed at the Englishman
when he plaintively disclosed that our women,
my sister-in-law, understood him
more than us, more than us men.

Out of fear I think, that nervosity,
the laughter of the thought of it
the very, very thought.
My God, this is close.

For ficksake then –
finger wagged in public
for waving at a girl I know
a free gift of my hello.

I'll take my phalanges
and throw them in his face
just to spite, spite?
just to spite history.

Think Nothing of it. Acha.

The first talk is stolen from media hacks
here and there who've spurted words
of dishonour for this man
and he's quick to re-birth the equilibrium.

It's all the Paki's he says
in Bradford, us Indians wouldn't do it
them fucking Muslims
fighting against the state.
As if I'd know nothing of it,
coming from there, that country.

And then I've had Ireland for breakfast,
for dinner and tea, more recently,
blood curdling and boiling and freezing
When I try to explain
a c i v i l   w a r
the word sticks like fresh putty
on a broken window pane.
Nothing registers beyond what's known.

No bullets in civility, only petrol bombs
and stones a few harsh words
and the whip of a stick
the loss of a car or commerce
and both sides agreed
walking through a pack of dogs
was never going to be easy.

The silver liveried lay out their table
while on All India we go live to interact
with correspondents, from the forty eighth
meeting of those heads - of state.
We shout at Kashmir and Pakistan Afghanistan
to make it plain, too scared to press the button

less its played and pressed here soon.
They recoil to diplomacy on the hill
search for cigars, for freedom in the four walls
of some pestilential democracy.

Voluntary Redundancy.

There is big change coming in a couple of months
and there might be an opportunity to employ
a manager.
But that's managing I say
just managing getting by.
Be our creative manager he says
be creative getting by.

We duel like this is our language
and have contemplated displays
We may say performance
related pay. We may dream
we will dance in the air
with a thousand angel bells
and laugh at the very thought of getting by.

For **Arvind – contemporary performer.**

Sally Forth and Richard Backward march in time to the never ending clock
Under the watchful eye of the naked distillery, dormant and docile
it's skeletal frame a reminder or rememberance
the comeuppance of a thousand karmic livers or more, bloated
expanded, corroded, disbanded.

Some of these exchanges were perilous Backward,
heed the call of the carrion crow.
In the rookery eggs were incubated
neighbours carried sticks to beat neighbours
the great defence of the nest offence of the rest.
There's a prescription in the handwriting Backward
and the masses won't have it.

ATV 1 : You have 156 new messages.
ATV 2 : to listen to your messages press one.

All this ferthepriceofacuppatea!

ATV 3 : to change your options on your drinks machine
press four.

I think for sure alot of these children are protected by poverty
from the trauma of the west, we have field officers to ensure
a complete synthesis with nature, after protracted negotiations.

4th ARCHBISHOP : What's the news from Warsaw?
5th ARCH :   I don't know but from where I'm sitting
the month's so bad we can't make babies
for rebirth.
6th ARCH :   When I'm at home I get visits from social marketeers.
3rd ARCH :   Feel at home.
6th ARCH :   Well, aren't you the charmin' brahmin.

The cottage industry took root here Sally, waiting for the compost.

Shook hands over the threshold of two homes
instead of stepping into the street.
The cricket hops across a world and lands on the wings of a
bright red butterfly - heading south towards the strings of an
Aeolian Harp. *(music)*

In the barrack room Richard Backward stirred his stumps and fell
headlong into the vernacular just in case borrowed money misfit the crime.
Sally Forth continues forward to the sound of the never ending clock

The Language of Drums.

To find the insolence in solitude
one must sit naked next to friends
who once sat laughing
 in the face of familiarity.
To forewarn of the nature of living
the nature of good, that beyond
the rhythm of the instrument.

The Ashram Gardener.

Halloween Pooja
when I mention the celebration
this devout man with green
fingers his mind for recognition
and remembering
at some child memory
and re-collection - and pain
in his face - the non
participation in the party plan
this mix and blend of light
and spirits, festivals, stories,
histories, herstories.
The final walking away
with light and faces towards
the dark warm night
is missing in him I think
as he toils away in his nursery.
Some Georgie Peorgie this is.

Rest

in these days of tumult
even Einstein, freshly risen, unkempt
cries in laborious leisure. must be so.
He carried this weight for so long
the gain of his existence
a precursor to the end. Pressure for sure.
His equation, finally finished
with a little sleep, sound
beyond matter, reason and life.

Shame.

After reading the newspaper on the 1st of the month
The carpet bombing begins in earnest
and still the street is asking for food
passers by stare on in amazement
at the continuance of this man
take photos without asking
for the tourist show back home
strangers shout my name from street corners
elevated to stations by being so low
I don't belong.
More travellers adhering to principles of trust
that might transmit signals to beating partners
Blue smoke rises from foreign lands
real-terrorists sit quiet and reflect
with street children, chided by the jealousy
of the drunken husband - street clean
and unkempt.

The Global Village Panchayat. *

The few are pulling the strings for themselves
and the obvious distortions everywhere
only benefit those given seats at the table.
For me, I'm sitting on the floor
Expecting more unrest for the best of them.

I distinguish some difference across the great divide.

*Panchayat - village elders' council.

08.45 eastern daylight time.

I am constipated
as the wtc goes bang
and down
remembering how
a conversation
about NEW YORK
going tits-up
like Rome before it fell.
A favourite of mine.
The bell-boy repeats
the word
terrorism?
I remember Caesar, history
and the rest of it.
I tell the manager that this is
the beginning
want to check out of room 616.
911? One two one two.

Monsoon Begins, barman sings.

At the end of a thin line of rope
mothers man-handle their children
from the rain storming relentless.
We have taken food from the floor
in the street with the homeless
invested big time in a no win situation
like it was ever a competition right?
reconciled ourselves to the race
the competition the all seeing I.

The weather changes, everything changing
and childless women now going grey
shiver in the chill warm winds.
Hanuman is having a field day
he blows east to west
amid an undue storm
life persists against good measure
while we wait for patience to abate.

Bar Bill.

see significance in everything
knowledge in nothing
less than a cup of tea
assiduously we listen to advice
upon advice, take lessons from angels
split infinities with blunt knives
carve our names in city walls
word gets round
and more and more people come
it's not in the guide
and certain people, start the gleaning.
I take no commission
But it's spreading
like anthrax in a dead envelope

Tamil Tambi.

The man who wears the Royal Oak Whiskey cap
now manages these boys, cooks the books
on a low heat and cries sometimes unabruptedly.
I learn of his history in the seminarium
how close to God he became
and where he is now
between marble and sandstone
counting figures underneath Visa,
The World's No.1.
In my country he sold the forest for the family
and could not see the wood for the trees
Held god for sadhana, came like a lion
escaped a thief, cursing the blessed rock
from whence he fell.

Still he gives the Blessing.

The man who would have been priest
preaching pub-like upon the nature of the beast.
I'm not knowing specifics, nor he
but know enough to know
this is why he's in the stable
and not the pulpit.
In these times it's hard or foolish, perhaps both
to know where to stand
leaving out standing around a table of discontent.

Three drums begin to round and bells ring beyond
bells are shaken and a guitar joins, strum
thin and unsure like fox cubs leaving a hole.
The total rhythm begins for the virgin girls
incense for the mind, spirit not foremost yet.

Arrack.

Behind the Arrack Shop, laid waste and undiluted only plastic,
hogs ravaging through less than protein, an overacreage of detritus
left for the toil of tomorrows men. It can only be seen,
this, this everything. Only to say, my friends
who form the circle of their own conformity
will not come here, behind the plastic of their rubbish.
Life at it's best and worse a curse
That begin, began, begun, begot.

Travelling before my Ticket.

As the train stops in cool morning sunshine
along side the track, keet hutted dwellings
wondering if shanty is peace, really dem I
while an old woman oils a young womans' hair
gently flicks clean a comb with a safety pin.
I'm yearning for some news
between the ticket inspector and tomorrow
a breath of air in this stagnant world pool.

At Basin Bridge the instruction coach
stands idle in the siding – teachers,
instructors have run for their lives.
This train carriage carries another bridge
across the tracks.
The world will see what this day brings.
In poverty no knowledge is golden, only
the threat of another days' tense vibration
looms this life.

Before

A hot day on Blackboy Hill
cruising down in neutral
on the radio only bird-song
in the whole of the car, the air
the aim a test transmission.
Chirrupping sonorous beauty.
Some years ago now is it?
Sweet as a bird on a wire waiting to fly south.

In an almost monastery garden.
(after Kettleby)

In the food preparation room
of a suburban guest-house
delightful in this peace and seclusion
the robust man-hating Tibetan kitchen queen
eyes me quizzically almost throwing blind knives
makes requests sound like orders to the maid, done.

She wears a back printed t-shirt-writing like this:
w e a r e a l l g o d s . Gods got in red.
I say to her man, be god to man
and if you can't be god be good.
She does not want to speak nor profers owt
just a kitchen conversation defence against her world
attack attack attack.

Human Unity Choir.

A request is made, emmissary sent
the cathedral is locked
there is nobody home
and the bishop has refused
the choir.
They are wanting to sing sacred but
someone has not kissed his ring.
He sleeps and the scaffolding
up for repair, remains in place.
Sirens call the siren call
and Romans will be sung tomorrow
with or without this holy child.
At the gates of this great temple
an eejit sits with his golden shroud
banging at the gates of a land locked
heaven.

Kandy.

We conjoin to remind ourselves of what we were
to confirm that which we lost by our own design
then we were worshipped as gods, today we are nothing
more than gods. The fact remains,
the world will see what terror brings,
before, when we remembered we were gods,
all of us gods.

the photographer saying I don't shoot poverty
the local saying but poverty sells to Europeans
the photographer saying it's a difficult one.

We relay a real time image to the world
and reflect back the image we think we see.
We would like to help, we really would
from both sides of a fence of equal green.
But, no but, what we see and what we share
we ask ourselves, will take us where.
What we are, beyond the fence
will stake our futures far from hence.

There is no him, there is no her
nor us nor them nor they nor we.
We have become, we must become,
we shall learn to know our poverty.

Advice.

He never gave advice he said, when he did
on that odd occasion, he nearly killed someone.
A child he said.
Every word that told a story, every
lie that became a myth.
When half truths walked naked
without shame with cold reason.

Eventually we sought
absolution from the truth
but it could not be rubbed out
taken away, defiled, maimed or broken.
It only stood, like a lantern
Beacon roaring out the light into
a darkness that screamed dry pride.

Those that foretold the future
told stories of how it began
How, like lions sleeping we all went
restless to our incarnate graves.

I heard you ask for this.

The best advice is given
only on intimation
and seeing as you asked
hearing as you asked
I proffer this
The money is already printed
so we can't make any today
or tomorrow
and the only time, so to say
is when the ink runs out,
then perhaps, we'll go from home,
to the field for a while,
or talk to the printer a little.
please
don't dispute my tacit sincerity
for counterfeit,
hold this law and pestilence.
The rat-catcher's note was due today
and the sun is already high
Crow-pecked mango stones are baking
on red terracotta floors.

Like this, in small town talk in this
sub-sectioned overview
development of the politest kind
is being questioned here
and a little subversion never hurt nobody
any body.
Who did you say you were?
Teacher, writer, critic, friend...
The day the curtains went up
pots were thrown or lay dormant
ready for the grand design.
The day we sold the universe.

After a letter.

In the hot afternoon we talk of love and things
with a constant I not understand. Between letter
writing and translation we communicate with parents
and further translate our regret at not sharing
maybe it's come the time to share. Stealing?
Retrenching into cultural traditions for me to be
her English teacher. Almost a joke. But not quite.
She'll learn this language fast. Sometimes it helps
but not quite. Taking back what you assume is yours.
The face is not happy when I tell her that she come.
relief and loss writ large on your face.
But the gutt reaction to a small joke
is to throw a dictionary in my face.
I think I'm other than the teacher,
but have not definitions only love turned sour.
And when I can't win the argument I say you say
it's not so important and walk out the door.

After School.

She has gone and we were a great school.
our curriculum sometimes determined by culture
sometimes by the reaction to the event as it happened
We even found physical education fun again.

In the maths class it was mostly her lesson
but what I lacked in algebraic equations
I bedazzled with the language of geometric behaviour.

At break times we talked of bunking off for tea
to our different cultures but knew the families
would never lay the table for the extra, the other.

In the playground, here's where we really learnt
that across the nets, under the trees
and all around the hop-scotch pitch
this is where we really learnt
when we were nerveless, when we were free.

At the commencing of the new school year
shall we be streamed together again.
I doubt it, these teachers know how potent it is
how together, in twos and talking groups
We could subvert this education all the way
to heaven.

From Dogma.

a postcard from the edge.

The dreaming Dolphin
is traumatised in sea blue.
There where you go
there give no way, trust instinct,
look the signals.
Have the power for doing the big jumped.
You must look what is right.
What is not right and who you are?
All dreams come true.
A dreamer never forgets the dream.
from this is what you make life.
From this is what you make Life.
dreams for your life,
very important just one dream.
Just this dream that keep she alive
some people not dream.
Difficult to dream. What's your dream?
You want tell me?

We begin again in our hapless happiness
a little introspective and wary of our words.
Speaking spoken dreams I know destroys
some feeling is broken like trust.
But we start again.
She will have her way.
The wash man's justice scrubbed hard
on this fine dogma's thread
and the silk of the filthy rich got torn
no wonder, half this sacred mountain cow
co-habits with the blue bird
who shares the wash man's basin.

You don't live your dream she says

in the judgement.

hear that word!
happy now?
Jagged justice and seductions.
When you're falling.
It's like painting something
in the image you're wanting to create
Like fever flushing out.

Then, having become, what to do. Continue.
The easiest to say the music removes my anger
and while I come not home drunk anymore
the very thought of a dictate from dogma
sends me reeling to the music.

House Rule Number One.
that your music go now, your learning
and understanding.
It cannot eat me more.
I shall only be, be, stammer, holden.
In the months to come your reflection
will burn holes in both our memories.
While perfect scars reveal a time once had.

Cross-words.

I return from our mid-weekend to solitude from the city
and search for words to clear the vision in my minds eye
of that which was of the moment in frenzied energy
to find a little of what is left of you, remaining there attacked.
The chorus still sings in rapture waiting for a solo
from a single wind instrument more than a voice.

For a short time I was a representative force
around an arranged table for your friends not relations
you gave me, to remember what is becoming in them.
I am the broken skin sung of in other worlds
for all to see what is behind the signs, the seeing.
In select neighbourhoods play stations are modern spinning tops.

We will sail up the river together for sure despite
the course we all agreed to construct when we began,
to see how the bend in nature was our own doing.
Only the shadows of jazz, silence between cabaret acts
striding off to change costumes in the night
will remind those concerned of the ever change going on.

A Female Peacock Struts Her Stuff.

We cycled from city to city in the early morning monsoon dew
smack in the middle arcing glow of a too vibrant rainbow,
promised ourselves more than the earth, that beyond violet.
Road stops for phone calls to a loving mother disguising the affair
and I'm sure in her voice she revealed the game, some small ecstasy.
Just before home that we cannot distinguish, turning street heads agog,
a change of shirt, assurance and work, we pass through a funeral
playing respects to the garlanded dead, offered coffee in the grieving
silence not mourning.

You slipped into breakfast service in the Ashram, for me
a roadside milk rich thick tea sufficed, amongst men
reading no new news of wars that shame this foreign tongue.
The strong may stand alone but the great sit down together,
together alone we tramp through life a god given right
they say is true. With new words this love my rock.
You wash and clean and offer me drinks, I now stand alone
and the band plays on to spirit away the dead.
Whistling away beauty never did any harm
today we have inherited the wind and charmed its' course.

Festival of Light to The Mother's Birthday.

Every syllable spoken is true, though some so inapplicable
I listen on every word for a release of herself from that
This is true beauty and so mixed upon this spirit thing
Some deep, deep sorrow seems immodest bitterness
gives way to some golden love an inner denial, surrender.
Together Alone We Talk.

As the morning sun burns my face awake
on the warming grass matted terrace bed a night of
sleeping above her dreams, the world is a cacophony
of crackers like carpet bombing a far off reflection.

She comes in white to say hello, the woman saves this man,
stooping in the shadow to give good mornings to this captive.
Cold kisses later and then unsure, some warmth, an entry back to life
A trust formed among the heartless storm.

Later, on the doorstep to needed sleep I wonder
how it is that it can be and turn so quick
the broken mind and bodied come with faint hellos
distraught, destroyed and somewhat lost
amidst this all, this everything.

And on the day the birthday came, strange rumours
play upon the mind, while they process and we proceed
the progress made may go to seed, we're hoping not
though in between we doubt some more
so begins the seven days of reticence, regret and more.
I mark this day.

Sunshine and showers.

Underneath everyone's statue I sit staring
at eight pillars of wisdom and an empty ice-cream cart
today is the first day of fifteen minutes of solitude
beside me sits an urchin with a wild runny nose
a smile to kill the plague of plagues.
Could be she sends spies for the checking, people pass
in a holiday mode, carefree, everyone an unsent messenger.
Rutted rainwater in the void between great men
dries quickly in the east coast heat.
The ice man mounts his cart for fresh stock.
Watchmen carry sticks for the trespassed
today we have run out of time.

Impatience with divinity.

I cannot wait and fall headlong to that room.
What's called spontaneity leads me up this garden path
and between the packing and explanation
steal her off to friends and heart that declared before.
Time out and shy is the verdict from the wise.
Beginning to see the mistake being made
pushing too hard for things I can't see
leads to madness, fact.
I can't help myself and need another
only goodwill and immortality saves this day
one hangs listless from a vine near the temple
another is impossible for we are mortal.
In the returning haste, I listen to the plea
this oh too beauty, some honesty
and in the room of indecision as she closes down
I throw ripped red roses to fulfil her wish
to clarify the intention once denied.
There are no more days like these.

Remission.

stop the drinking stop the smoking
use soft words and voice like velvet
stroke the patient with pure linen
Listen to this pillow talk
(with a pinch of salt to soil sheets)
Take gravy with it for digestion
Believe nothing that the caged bird sings
These her only iron bars to file.
She cannot know what this is for.
Late this morning after last night
not know what comes all through the door.

I cannot tame these demons, angels
corrupted by some thing mild,
In the up end of this cul-de-sac
no more of anything left or right
freedom fighting, simply nothing, naked sleeping
on terrace floors,
waiting for the end prescribed.

Intermission.

we spend the day together and argue politely
after we agree a difference, but the same
you say, tonight there is no respite
to your need, a home, some place to sleep.
However you suggest coming tomorrow,
you do not know what I lose, what we
m i g h t   h a v e   h a d
but I am poor you see
and the rich come, normal beyond
the doubt we are not supposed to have
we are complacent, not knowing our neighbours needs
cannot recognise we could piss on them
If we knew how.

Hasya, Karuna, Vera.
Very Down to earth.

In the house of reconciliation
on anniversary end pooja day, music plays
and a very long alap
the rhythm begins to return
while younger acolytes listen like yoga
returning travellers find their days
full of impassioned glory, some still obstinate
to the great rhythm of it all
one man sits in too solid pain
could not see the light gone out, opposite
music stops at the end of truth.

Obstinate Persons Retreat.

After blessing the bike with a mozhum
of purple, orange a touch of green
Someone comes to go
all this after saying I stay
I do not go. She goes. Walks out.
My young friend tells me
I perform great social service.
Yes, this has been some performance
and me the ruthless editor
translator of realities
creator of dreams.

Saru.

The leaves are still hanging. Green.
The sky a deepest purple against an imagined black sea.
There is no moon nor peace in the park living room
no wind but not stifling. People come and go.
Occassionally a hooter from vehicles pierces serenity.
Walking towards the hotel there are many thoughts.
Walking towards the hotel I think of you.
Everything else is lost, everything else is unreal.
Tonight you cannot be on my mind, I think.
You are far from here, also. Yet you are here.
I have missed winters in the slow change of seasons
given oil to the watchmans' wick and still
Still the leaves are still hanging, still. Green.
The sky a deepest purple against an imagined black sea.

one two three.

We sat in the succour of materialism, the bustle
of the great cathedral, stained glass dedications to consumerism
the twenty first and last century to spill its' split beans.
I thought we were in for a weekend retreat, both running
far far away from contrite responsibilities. Didn't even think.

You know, I never met a woman who wore a sari so badly.
Even on the day she moved in with her mother. Invited just once,
it was clear I would never get on in the maternal and she'd wear jeans.

Everything was planned but the shock sharper than a surgeon's knife
in the split second of telling a lifetime passed before me
like news of a close friend's death, which it would have become.
It's no longer possible to deceive nature I note, having run it's course.

Nine months from now in the Autumn that will not come
I shall remember this day for it's passing, how,
amid the plastic and chaotic exchanges of sin
we continue to turn life off. The choices made beyond the sales floor
at the top of our elevator, cannot be sold.

Womb Ablutions.

On the way to scheme a reuniting of a child with its mother;
an exasperated kidnap plan across continents
on the weekend, planning, I consent to abort mine, generally
an-aesthetically, like aesthetics counted right ?
Everyone is so polite and too an untouched button
this that all would suggest is true, standing on a balcony
the opposite of an expectant father, still still nervous.
Here an action opposite creation, Sunday morning
all motion set perilously in reverse.
What remains are receipts for a clean job done and a scan
Scraped and flushed away meticulously.
An abnormality was agreed upon, an excuse borne for the mother
who will never be, this time round.
I travel further for redemption, convention
More motivated than a time before. Before.

A little later some confidence is betrayed
and the word is out at this loss, bereft
the shining spirit of a lost truth bleeds on
through the shimmering glimmer of the immortal.
Our bedroom caper comes a cropper proper,
an acid scrape and it is done
Small change from another world
passing swiftly over to the next.
We have only to tip the nurse now
and move slowly home to rest.

Black Pearl Permit Room.

Some attempt to reveal myself :
Everyman has some volatile potential
yet the agreement with the soul
(if one cannot already agree with the self)
should come from the next, which is outside
and mediated on by the other force;
That which we deny by the subliminal arrogance of self.
First this, then more.

Beside the eyes that pry beyond the truth we are
that sees nothing, not even stars from whence we came
We only see the gaze of some others contention
the match – the fight – the result of which
We may only answer to ourselves –
a union of the great divinity within us.

After this, this day that cursed and told
the truth of modern urbanity, I cannot see
wood for the trees, the truth behind that smile.

From the moment of conception
to the second we abort
the product of emotion
was the nature of the thought.

Enchanting the Producers' Daughter.

spell bound on this journey
being inclusive in this life
for the length it takes a train
between two stations, and a little sleep
we jostle our verbs around babies
and children
playing doctor's and nurses
on the railway bank through many stations.

Sapna.*

In the shadow of the sapna
the fat producer sleeps
behind the Maitre d' – maitre don't.
A beef cake of incredulity, B – Movie star
wanders, flexing his chest
and shifting his ego.

Behind the shot, blind justice
stands alert, a grape
and cigarette butt
tilting the balance of her scales.

Beyond the horizon
harmonised water from the spirit shop
helps Sapna dream
and understand the spirit mentality –
solitaire, palm top, all the way
from the US of eh ?

The Real Terrorist –
We wake up laughing
like sober stoics
stirring up Pan to frighten Zeus.

* *sapna – dream.*

Filming potential.

Greed or desperation pushed them to it
an ageing teacher says she could get rich
in a half a year, she's bitterest
ney - mardy, a word so colloquial even
dogs refuse to bark at it.
This child like anger that will not go
until love rears its ugly head
like throwing bombs at the untimely dead.

Red. Yellow. Black. White.

can mean the bloodshed
of the heroes
who stand for freedom
for the oppressed
and the oppressor.
the colour of the earth.

for someone who knows
who can make something
out of the frustration
or disturbance.
a yellow bird on a green leaf.
the wealth of the land.

can mean the people
their good future
an attitude of mind
spirit.

Mbyani.

a spare elastoplast.
He runs off in search
in search of another battle
Pride in his heart
blood on his leg.

T - SHIRT thoughts.

THE REAL TERRORIST

GLOBAL VILLAGE - rape and pillage

CEASE FIRE EXTINGUISHER

WHAT DEM MEAN ?

ONLY LOVE - and egg dossa

COKE ? ANTHRAX ? - up your nose

TURNING WORDS
just turning ficking words

JOKE'$ over

NO MORE JOKE!
more than some
less than others

COMEDY , KOMEDIE
(any funny event)

'We acknowledge and bewail our
manifold sins and wickedness
and are heartily sorry.' Prince Charles.
Like fuck we are.

repeat in Tamil, Telegu, Malayalam, French
and the Queen's english
all hand painted of course.

Thursday and the Supramental. West.

Spring into Summer
This year the Marathon will run
on grass unseeded on homeland turf
whilst new birds' nesting prove their worth.

Zeus blows through the Olive Grove
to remind me that his wife is here;
I eat gold corn from Heras' field
remove chewed chaff with po'light hands
have sucked stolen cherries from her tree
Certain of the path I tread
but let's see how far the gods will go.

Hooglin and Mooglin sit erect, they teach
to watch and report from the Cypress trees.
A significant scaffolding offers rest
to moss-mouthed birds who try to nest
(a crack appears in the Apostles' head)

Foregone the fishing with good friends
to do the duty on my foreign soil
Drink with men licking piss off thistles, yes.
This my home with Gods indeed.

I have found the spring
and washed my feet
again and again and again
Hera, she goes, see how she goes
She gone she gone she gone.

Trouble.

I am that goat of lunar festival speak
driven here by the wind from Aeolus' mouth.

I throw two stones like one at a chanticleer taunt
one on that way up, another is coming down.

I am painting stains and the sign on the bench
in the fireplace reads WET, blanket, bench, PAINT.

There will be trouble, only two people read it
a masseur enquiring for my well being
in the guise of explaining her own unwell;
and a campbloke giving a course in the big-room
about loss and grief with casual gay abandon.

Rose petals have been put in a bowl of water
in the fireplace, far away from the wet bench.

A goat-boy wears red on the hillside
picks himself nimbly through the sage
with a crooked stick in his hand
ever the surveyor of homeland turf.
Rests beneath this tree see, the root of
an island world, made steady by the hand
of an unmasked god.

Joker.

The woman who warns against past lives
is shagging a pious church warden
and feeling great. He declaims Mother Theresa
in a radical conversation. Do It Anyway, he says.

I may take this opportunity to offer my head
to the hunters, do it anyway, hunting oh so
politely. To dance like a deer through the trees.
Taqdeer.

Polite society conversation.

Talking about what is clean and what is not,
powerful stuff for the pathfinder.

Have you noticed how dirt looks dirtier
in a plastic bag.

The dangers of being pure in a toxic world
anything that is natural is couched
in the fire-place.
Take some time for people to catch up
slowing down. Upside down thinking,
forward planning, backward thinking
backward planning forward thinking
innocent amazement.

How the morning begins.

A donkey chewing hortha in the olive grove
a reprimand for computer use
a memory of a sailor talking of freedom
an old woman dressed in black, widow
tapping her stick down the hill.

Fresh flowers for the writers' room
a communiqué to a boss in apology.

The water is cold so paying guests
will not be happy at the trudging
up the hill for scrubbing and learning.

This I know, that teaching is a subtle
thing and those that lead
get burnt first.
The donkey will have its' weight to bare
but for now there's time to chew
some cud.
The farmer's field far off
begins to turn from brown to green.

Before work.

Like yoga, qui gong, meditation
nasal salt baths and waking up
I get to be with myself
before the coffee goes on and down.

Carrion sea-birds feel safe enough
to eat on the other side
of my window in the shelter
given by the courtyard on the hill.

Workmen descend on petrol donkeys
those uncoughed carrotless beying animals,
to begin the day at another's door
whilst gods talk to me
on the radio shackled to a monastery
shifted to the other side
of the onion field.

We are all lovers
I feel the force of everyone.

Tuesday, again.

I often begin Christ-like
though more rarely now
knowing the people still
won't put up
with it.
To save my own sacrifice
or portend a crucifixion
I drink Apostollo wine
and heavy bread.
It helps to pass the day
as the sheep keep bleating
on a petty beourgeoise hill.

Coaching New Beginnings.

the smart psychiatrist says I'll be alright
she's here to flog a book on love and share theory
and I ask myself why the world trainer, capital based
and fully ensconced in united nations relief endeavours
would want to offer life coaching
to a once pronounced renaissance man
if she did not want to learn about herself.

I am the second generation man
this time round
to be dragged up on feminist war theory
have fought the battle over and over again
yet, still I feel the piss in my face.

this morning I will smell of goat
and decorative flowers will pick themselves.

Dr. Eam. Medicine Man.

carries the weight of the world
in his sleep. An Herculian sleep
binding continents with unstuck compassion.
Bubbles of nocturnal thought unbinding fear.

He prescribes happiness as an antidote
to the common complaints in his practice.
A general generous practitioner
as he unlocks his medicine cabinet
the music falls out, into the light.

He calls Hippocrates to attention
wears his voice out on the end of a stethoscope.
'I have had a dream past the wit of man'
to say what medicine that was.

Genderless Bed Contract.
to be signed in the kitchen

I have come here of my own free will
having been mutually enchanted thus far
without duress or discontent.
I am happy to be here.

In the event of subsequent regret
I   the kitchen keeper
of any responsibility towards that regret
and remove him/her of any fiscal
emotional or practicable personal
associations arriving from this event
should he/she wish to do so.

In the signing thereof
I am in my right mind
and also of a consensual attitude.

Signed.
Date.

I drop a contract into the coven, to see.
It seems they too have learnt that
Men are dry mouthed
de-preciated and damaged too.

Bedrooms are for meditation
making babies
and keeping mum.

Global Transient Amnesia.

Smashing time to sleep through the storm
he went on through the silent lands
the night, whilst it happened elsewhere.

In the day a siesta with neighbours
the cynic the nervous chatterbox
and a chain smoking anaesthetist.

A lady comes to teach us balance
dressed in fine chiffon and jeans
what it is and how to profess, practicing.
Her ribs are broken, pelvis bent
she has come to teach balance.

Holistic London Underground.

Leicester Square
probation officers

Regents Park
merchant bankers

Kentish Town
owner occupiers

Royal Free
Patients

Skyros Central
holiday makers

Tuffnell Park
realists

Bedlam
dreamers

Piccadilly
lost boys

Oxford Street
consumers

Crouch
End
family.

Light on Water.

There is a rareness of space
that is mine
and objectively undefinable
like the shimmer of changing colours
on a receding Aztec path
made possible by a sinking sun
flashing one time green, another purple
yellow orange and blue
yet always within that spectrum.
The variations are damnable and glorifiable both
only to me because.

Natural Forces.

The hand that writes the word
mightier than the implied sword, is bitten
and swollen beyond the wrist. Left.
It's no surprise is it, that nature
takes it's course to remind
the power-full or the path-finder
just how much ink it takes
to change the state.

Tales from New Reality.
(a small village on the edge of Human Unity)

Fuck you politely, I did stay in luxury
for one night after you left me
September 11th, now there's a day
me standing alone with the world.
But, (this word a dis-ease) I did it
to research the extra for you.

I always tasted friction first
or dipped toes in hot oil
to save you blistering your feet.

The ambassador for the Christ.
after a painting by Paula Rego.

Comes and shares a truth
not the truth, you have that
man, he lays on the hands
calls it like it is.
He comes, see how he comes
towards the dawn, tomorrow.

Tense.
date as postmark

from here you can see the future
it is not written on parchment or pigskin
onion paper like those dissident blokes back then
it is in the sky, in the unreason of the dead
who will rise to claim their stake
on the grieving world.

Vacation.

two old lovers, reconnoitered
wander together, lost in wondering
being in their reclaimed space
passed on not seeing and seeing
they have come home
for a time.

One way or another
we are all going home
or choose
to sail away.

Touching the Goal.

I do it

not by halves

Go the whole hog

deliver the goods

Make short work

of bringing home

the bacon

I am as good

as my words.

Well, he seems very cap

able.

Sterile.

Integral yoga is antibiotic for chickens
intensively farmed for a jalfreezi market
you'd never know the tartrazine in it.
How the wishbone stripped clean
before the twist and the crack
pips the cockerel's dreams to the nest.

I not I.

hungry
angry
lonely
tired

Stop the ire
Halt the I.

On the back of Henry Thoreau.

A bee is fooled embarrassed by plastic foliage
how nature has been cheated by man's folly.

In the village I'm told it takes two days
For brandy to wear thin in the blood
and twenty seconds to re-enter the pin
on a mobile phone gone awry somehow.

Grief takes two days at least, I notice.
We have negotiated our vulnerabilities
Re-invented the wheel for the race
proved peace abounds on the inside somewhere
the worm will turn having forgotten the soil.
Things die.Things are dead. That's true.
A new life is in the offing, upping
in the woods, something has begun.

Taller than.

I dump the agenda
one prescribed week ahead of myself
with half a calendar in the fireplace
three rough diamonds masquerading as bliss
two cut edges from a vine
and a replacement peace vase from above
fine brazilian crystal before
the effortless removal of self
from   -   the firing line.

History mostly records the victor's records
accepting the conceding and the turning
the back on the battle, walking away,
stronger, walking tall.

**The End of the
Contractual Game.**

Actually, the conflict negotiator
and the plumber from the Glaswegian slum
the this and the that, don't give a fuck.

For this is monkey business
and whilst I a monkey
I woke and smelt daisies,
geraniums, saw the olive getting fat
even before the dogs and bitches
pre-tended to bleat or bark
their bar-king ting to the world.
Some corporate nonsensedisguise.
C-c-c-courses for horses and their
bitter fucked up post modern
trans national masters.

Accident Book.

canine bite
the participant was nipped by a bitch
as she climbed a hill to The Crystal Tree,
often referred to as the Joshua Tree
more recently known as The Judas Tree.
Oh, Jonah. All trees for all men
and dogs it seems.
She did not wish to have the bite-scratch reported
as she considered it prejudicial to her escort
and to time spent more freely without the confines
of the constructed community.
The escort advised a tetanus upon return
to her native country and subsequently
cleaned the broken skin with sterile wipes
and pure pure alcohol.
It is to be noted that the participant is fearful
of the female dog and this was sensed
by most living things on the ascendant climb.

Paradox.

Ms. Walker lost her balance whilst on the final steps
of the short walk to see the monument to Immortal Poetry.
She grazed her left knee
and complained most politely of previous injuries
to her ankles during other falls
the week before arriving for her holiday.
She was a little shocked and declined assistance
of support on the downhill walk to the centre.
She enjoys a drink.
A facilitator remonstrated with the walk leader
for pushing the elderly too hard
and administered an arnica tablet to relieve the shock
and apparent pain.
The walk leader cleaned the grazing with cotton wool
and hydrogen peroxide solution.
Ms. Walker suggested she change her name
and requested the wound be left open
for the healing.

Greek Gods at their Airport.

I'm sat at the airport having abluted
in the disabled toilets and thought about
sexual discrimination, staring down
the end of along Corbusier tunnel –
architect dreamer, to a red light
occasionally blue, never green.

The police come to check
an abandoned taxi, cuss-to-mer-less:
it could be littered with bombs, who
knows. They prance
around and pass pieces of paper.
Eventually a lithesome one puts a note
underneath the wiper blade on the screen.

In the language of the gods
it most probably reads:
'We know you have a bomb in there
and ask yourself most politely to remove it.'

To be sure, I have made cuttings
of the first Olive tree the Olympiads
will see this year.
It is folded in a red lunghi once used
to civilise an immortal poet.;

Had he shouted more often than I
when bit by mosquitoes, who knows
there may never have been a statue
there at all.

Writer's Blick.

Like block
But bigger.

Certain Death.

Between me you and the gate-post
(almost certainly granite that post)
my publisher has a big chin
and a white dog called Julie,
almost certainly beset with learning
difficulties, the dog.
He enjoys disturbing his sleeping wife
with poets dragged from the street or bar
(indeed she left him yesterday and both he
and the dog are distraught and melancholic.)
He can spin with the rest of them
taking my words from nowhere
and putting them in complete
a non-commercial antitdote to
anyhow, I was in this bar doing the me
myself and I and in walks Flynn…

Shy Poets.

are a verse
to recitation.

Mary, Mungo and Midge.

Vishnu comes to bring me coffee
Shiva comes to wipe my brow
Ganesh offers solitudes silence
while Kali donates deaths' knowhow.

Writing.

three a day like vitamins
suck and chew then swallow.
Above the cloud
above the dove
I suck and chew
then swallow.

For Tori.

I'll pen three a day like valium,   promise
so you can read yourself   when off
run around your receptors   without
that pressure that, strikes you   to believe
at twenty weeks those babies   don't hear music

And that's no judgement   believe
me I give seminally   nothing
taught myself to do so   except
occasionally, like a fucking   flowing river
disseminate our destruction.

Laboratory like   labor
mavericks will escape   the order
(applause like you've never been born)
at the front   we format
never closing the deal.

Automatic Writing.

has no clutch five gears
overdrive and wakes you
engine roaring in the night
the middle of the night
like a lorry driver beginning shift
to beat the traffic or get the bread
or Kenyan broad beans
delivered on time.

slowly in first sometimes
others full throttle but always
speedingtowardsthedestination
towards the morning out of mind
the little castellations and a pit stop
on the tarmac superhighway
stop.diesel.petrol.food,
daylight, action, movement
sleep.words.

An Arrid english English Lesson.

When I told the assistant manager
to cut off his tie
and stick the other half
up his arse. I was teaching english
Historical English
and I did it for you.

When I opened my wallet
and shared everything
except bus tickets
I collect for fresh wallpaper
I was teaching English
Modern English
and I did it for you.

When I wrote to the manager
commending his assistants' professional
conduct during a time of great pressure
I took off my tie
and cut it for you
Smiling at the snip, teaching me English.

The English Lesson.

private tuition continues unabated twenty four hours a day
for approximately twenty one days, give or take the odd
retreat for convalescence from this dictionary.
The content and form of the language is more than words
the action, reaction and change, too much, too fast, too soon
bends the motion of this teachers' creativity. Lessons stop
For now. Principals may institute a new semester, perhaps.
But for now the student is suspended. Somewhere
high on a roof top trying to plead a case for more study
From eh to zed not one more word. This teacher's tired,
bereft once besotted with the impartition.
Seems the more we give the more we get knotted.
close down these centres of learning, tick tock.

Sacresanct on the road.

Two cows
preceed
the poor cows
lost
it seems
but then, following
the sacred
we whistle in the wind
and laugh too much.

Religious Ferveur.

chorus:
To create
we wait
to change
the state
of things
to come
thy will
be done.

Fire crackers outside the temple
and Gowri tells me God is coming.

Bumper Sticker.

Jesus was an Oil Magnate.

If you get this
you're halfway
to making
a prophet.

Global Internal Combustion.

To drive the engine, to push the train
we burnt the coal
and acid rain
kicked the soft underbelly
of a small dog.
The automobile is a pleasure to drive.

No Blood for Oil.

the spoils of war
ease the emptiness of sorrow
long to come mr. President.

Oi ! 'TS Eliot' Get off the Stage.

I am nervous hungry and alert
as the group begins to co-convert
into electric and into the night
whilst sarcasm cuts like rotten blight.

Sawhney thinking through political elation
we take this train to another destination.
Thru' the fields and up the hill
we struggle for the sake of ourselves.

In the coffee shop, afterwords,
the anti symphonic chatter
blends with the music
for our re-creation.

Care.

Prefers much light
o' direct sunlight

water regularly
must not dry up.

Fertilise now.
and then…

Not Love Poem.

Red on green is black   *(echo)*

is the colour

of my true loves' hair.

ack   ack   ack   *   *(voice)*

*like gattling only sweeter
for voice, percussion and electric effects.*

The threat of reconciliation.

Fully drunk I slam into you
who say I am too much
you cannot cope nor cannot see
my love, my hope, my misery.

Quality.

two nuns in a tut – tut
white habits, brown skin
speeding to a destination
running towards their jesus
going home, homeward bound
knowing exactly where they're
coming from.

ten scientologists move into
a once happy bar, two months
bringing religion and relief
to a tsunami victim or two,
laughing all the way to the bank.

882. Aristophanes 30.

I am in his library
while you share his room
the books I read owe comedy some
and wise men in wisdom frames
bear fruit of birth
over acts of war
cracked and sweet like frozen chocolate.

(for Dipu on his birthday)

44.

I've been intimated
inculcated
incubated
and distressed.
made indifferent by taste
and chastened by the post-man.

Salad Dressing.

I know it's time to split the country
when cress
becomes 'hot and spicy salad garnish'
not cress, which is what it is.
Salad.
When we call what has always been
something other.
I quit.

'The 4th World War.'

I didn't know my neighbours 'til we met in the street
until we decided to not be afraid:

"Corporate civilisation through fear, through terror.
The Government says there are no problems here,
the Government says we are at peace.
The Government is at war and they have given it to us.
Us and them? Corporate globalisation.
The loss of national sovereignty, transnational corporations dividing wealth.
Working people are very vulnerable to the global corporations.
Fragmentation, isolation, fear. Speaks genocide with the quiet words
of an attentive technician. Basta , basta , basta .
Structural re-adjustment. I'm a field nigger in the city.
'These days I'm happy to have nightmares……'

Sitting amongst Thatchers' Children, not those described
by T. Griffiths some years ago at the Old Vic.
This is the morality of the world.
There are no ethics in the prevailing morality.
'Where are the nuts from, I bet they're from Iran'.
The peace accord is an essay on disappointment.
We organise outside the system.
My father was an independent observer in Palestine,
he didn't work for anyone. Like fuck he didn't.
Just like parts of Sheffield.

The 'You're all a bunch of Thatcherite Cunts!'
cleared the room of ladies
But not before he left the room first.
'Well, it's One World One Struggle'
the kids scream for pleasure outside the door.

Casting for Cash.

1. A black actor, non specific m/f.
2. An Asiatic actor, non English speaking m/f.
3. A one legged differently abled actor.
4. Two differently abled big men (one indigenous English).
5. A dog (or somesuch pet centred animal) no donkeys.
6. Three musically challenged musicians.
7. One physically challenged acrobat circus type.
   (must not be a dog)

A director
A stage manager-ess imperatively
One film maker
A designer of international repute

An actor comes with a list and a book source
of all to read concerning the unwilling and oppressed,
himself still comodified to victimhood
and selling himself well.

I wonder how and why history might be
remembered. My history, your history
all of it, and then ?

The world's car park is a pink elephant
in a room blue and getting fatter.
Victims, all shades sizes and vicarious persuasions
are preparing an assault on the status quo.

Escape.

at the port of indifference
the sweat gets in your eyes
and the arched rib of a spined
inter-national t-shirt
does the ring of changes

Peter Handley

Downsideup.

We lefties can still play social justice
You can guarantee, there's no spin here
abouts

Red Ken has resigned to drinking
in the wing tavern with no marks
They throw a blown game atta new moon
came out laughing at history
still pissing on the poor

My unscripted descripted opinion is this
The centre right concensus gknaws
it's blood soddened foot

We have walled in our dereliction
put windows on our bars.

Growing fat on soured milk
the constant contradiction is
the thickness of the silk.

Not the Answer.

Maybe, sometime, someone, will
explain to me, what I must do
apart from social work for people
like me and the rest of them
I mean
beyond the drums.

s u c h   r o u n d e d
q u e s t i o n   m a r k s

At a gathering to celebrate a coupling
I decide to keep face
and on the back of 'out of order'
follow the party, down the river
upstream and into the sun
with jazz behind me leading.

It's never been my position
to be at the back of the boat but
we all decided against the regiment
that is just stags on tour for a night.
The urge to jump and drown
is as strong as the valium offered
deferred for something bigger
than this
and this
it's not pretty, not serious.

Even the musicians deny me something
in their eyes, some loss, some ember of it all.

The Exhibition.

A : It's a nice picture. I need satisfaction
I need to know what the subject matter is.

B : Narrative is not important unless you want to say something.
For a picture to say something it needs to have clues.

Do we talk of surprise or the inevitability of fear and pity?

A teacher is the blind man's bluff
the politician the devil's anvil
your mother is of all sins your own
and yourselfs are under your skin
the statistician makes the bargain again
and authority sucks he said
authority sucks and I begin
under your skin to begin under
your skin he said is to start again.

Memo from the Ministry of Roads.

You are to be advised
That owing to the unfortunate demise
and recent extinction of the pelican bird
inter-path walkways dissecting vehicular
carriageways will henceforth be known as
Zebra crossings,
until such time as the extinction
of the aforementioned species.
At which point zebra crossings
will be known as
multi-racial pedestrian access routes
until such time as the extinction
of the aforementioned species
at which point…

Ellie's Wood.

We were left to be nature natural
moving forward on a road to a wood
untaxed without stress, insured without policy
unkempt, like it matters.
no scaffolding for time to hang upon constructed
knowing we were going somewhere
towards a light shining in the grey mist
of seasons' change and stasis.

Between the county border signs a hinterland of knowing
always between the borders I notice progress made
never on the line with apologies and approbation
getting lost in the getting there, forgotten November fog
still and aching in the silence it creates.
A dull consideration an antipathy to life
not under the weather but somewhere in it for once.

Past Brill's Farm, a curl of smoke from cosy chimney stacks
on Folly Lane crows stand sentry like on sleeping swine
content to doze idle in this black rich earth.
All this for the remembering of a not for nothing life
not long nor short but perfect in her simplicity
full stopped by what we tell ourselves is sleep.

The telegraph lines seem to take us there
our own morse code to decipher in the doing
almost as if we prompt ourselves, in the woods
soaring together, to where she sleeps smiling.
In the air and underfoot, something so intangible
verging on grace is it I believe.
her laughter from beyond I hear
an angel glance to soften fear.

On the Beach, sur La Plage.

I am here at the dog end of decadence
on the beach with the Europeans
all butt naked so the lifeguard regards
from his jet ski fifty metres off.
A topless woman sagging tits on a phone
talking I presume to the city beyond
a couple in front wrapped gloriously
around each other sharing their own dream
under a seasonal gesture from the sun.
packing, unpacking kicking sand in our faces
the burnt are burning still amidst joyful cries
of freedom for this sniff of a time.

Above the sand-dunes and a green flag
permitting entry into a still cold sea polluted pond
the car-park crammed with every plate
that shares the secret of this holiday geography.
They march off en famille with umberellas, towels
grass mats, cooler boxes, the kitchen sink
and the promise of the night remembering the sun
as it burns, burns, burns their living skin.

After dinner, into morning
when our given days begin again
allowing us the luxury of wallowing limpless
hoping for the burning sun again
to dissolve the memory of an after thought
and the whole knowledge that we must go home.

An Island 2024.

today a small group of 185,000
people calling themselves Anglo
Saxons live in an area some 15 miles
square, walled in by a high wire
perimeter fence somewhere south of
junction 23 on the M5 motorway near
the old city of Birmingham.
They serve to remind us of the old Jewish
integrity of loss, victimhood, community
the nascent hostility towards change
and progress for humanity.

Hostel.

the client

the secret tragedy of self mutilation.
you've got so much pain in your head
that you feel you've got to get pain
to relieve the pain. I was traumatised
as a child. I'm keeping that to myself.
Pain and hurt inside me. Using a razor
brings me relief. When you cut yourself
you're aware of what you're doing until
you cut yourself and then you black out.
It's not attention seeking.
It's what I've been through. It's my secret.
I'll cut myself at least once a day. But
when I'm stitched up I feel dreadful
that someone has had to stitch me up.
I go back and do it again because I feel
I'm such a bad person. I'm loved
don't get me wrong but what happened
to me has changed how I feel about me.
I don't like me. The past is the winner.
There's days when you can just reach out
for the razor to relieve the pain. It's so easy.
Bloodletting. The bloody Greeks did it.
I can withdraw into myself with a razor.
A mate of mine was a punk in the seventies,
he's gotta fucking great scar on his chest
between his fucking nipples, right across here.
It says 'sid vicious'. Amazing. Fucking amazing.
I'd spend a year in a psychi' hospital
and get sectioned if they'd only supply me
with razors. It's like alcoholism. Sometimes
the release isn't enough and I'll rub salt or
turpentine in the cuts just to feel the pain
more. Yes, that pain. Yes.
The temptations always there. To release

the pain in my head. Ah could blame me mam
or me dad but… I get isolated. Feel on me own.
Am I ill ? Is this a twenty four hour illness.
Someone said I have to learn to like myself.
I know that, but the release.

the project worker.

I'll not do it again. You must be fucking joking.
I've been doing seventy or eighty hours a week
fer them cunts. No, you've got to be joking.
I'd finish at about ten in the morning. Wait
outside a pub for a beer, t' get out of it.
No counselling after a night on, so you've got
all this inside. Taken all this negative energy
with nowhere to put it. Fucking hell.
So you have a couple of pints and troll home,
hit the sack for a couple of hours and yer back
at work. Peeling potatoes or opening twenty
eight tins of European intervention beef, the stuff
they can't sell legitimately, for dinner. No,
you wouldn't catch me in there again.
I've been beaten twice. Once I was out cold.
Stone cold. He threatened and I don't like threats.
So, I said go on then do it. Do it. And he did.
Out cold. Been walking around this city with a
death threat for three weeks. This other fella
threatened to shoot me if he ever saw me again.
For throwing him out. He wouldn't put his scag
in the sin bin for the night. The rules is rules.
Not much to ask, but needles and shit lying
around for people to trip up on. High as a fucking
kite amongst a bunch of drunken lowbeat unflying
kites. It's not playing ball is it ?

the volunteer.

I can't say why I started to work there.
I'd got this project going in a derelict room

above a pub. Anyway, it needed decorating
and I'd noticed at the bottom of the street
this other derelict building, this sheet of ply.
Big full on sheet. It was going begging,
so to speak. So I knocked on this door and
haggled for this sheet and this fella turns up
to be a project worker in this cold weather
shelter. Gets chatting, I offered to help.
Volunteer, I still can't say why. Perhaps
I've been following in my father's rather
large footsteps. He always gave a donation
at Christmas. I always thought this
commendable. That charity thing. Now
I'm not so sure. Charity. Culture.
Charity culture. It kind of creates it's own
sub-culture of dependency. Doesn't empower
anyone. Still the same old hierarchies.
Us and them. Givers and receivers. S'funny.
I met an old chap in a pub, he was telling me
there are only two kinds of people in this world
givers and takers and sharers and spenders.
Something like that. He gave me his newspaper
at the end of his pint. It made me wonder,
news of the world.
And when you're in there, you're shit. Literally,
see this is the only time when they've got any
power, sway over anybody, anyone else.
When they're in Hotel Paradiso. I want this.
Give me this, do this, do that. I'm not even there
to help you know. Just to. I don't know what.
Why would anyone want to subject themselves
to violence, arrogance, tempers, mental instability,
scabies, drug addiction alcohol addiction, all of it.
The bottom of the pile. But in a funny kind of way
I enjoy it.

Peter Handley

The Plough.

Most nights, stood staring
at what might look vacant
I spy strange mysteries
in the dark black sky

tonight the plough
above my head instead
of straight in front and up
displays the furrow
in the dark black sky.

Home Town Talk.

they speak in a tongue
I cannot understand
and I come fom here

Now you talk of rain
on the most lazy days
twice since Christmas
and rain on the windows

this familiarity
is closer than the wind
mightier than the word
stronger than the sun.

It would never happen in Africa
that place, that much I know.
To be rebuffed.
You sit down in a place
and you say hello-no refusal,
rebuffal of recognition
It's shared when we are one.
Except that we are not
and then it sticks

The French and more come here
to make instruments for the world
and see the disformity of us all
on this island, the centre, racing.
If you have become, then,
climbing into bed
with the great and the good, well,
there's nothing wrong with
barking at the dog

that chews your throat.
Is there?

Flyover, under.

A dull grey afternoon
wandering across the marsh by the river
towards the motorway, not for the motorway
but for the walk among horses, grazing thin fields.

Under a flyover of an orbital road
burnt out cars, illittered beer cans
peppered with air gun holes.

Graffitti in yellow and red, black, proclaiming
some blighters' territory on the concrete pillars
holding up the traffic going nowhere over head.

A flock of seagulls, sixty or more circling
ducks in drake mallarded company and the more
I spy magpies in the bare winter trees, the white tips
of tail feathers in the bush, a whole village larking
more than the lark, a confederacy of magpies
coming and going forty fifty I count each one
watching out for the other in the purple
of sleeping silver birch.

Three boys appear with a gun on a gate post
and all is gone.

We Were all at Sea.

Remembering on a cold Sunday
walking out along the coast
to the top of that cold country,
Before Norway, mountains, hoj fjells and snow,
Our feet washed by contrary tides

from the east, an answer
from the west, an answer
and from within us all, the truth
Two seas, and then some, rolling in together

Caught by the wind, the chill
the all gathered presence of grace
All together, all alone

Wrapped in thoughts of our own
independence, against the prevailing wind.

History gathers momentum hereabouts.
How that memory binds us now

Into the past, the future
belonging to all of us
the very nature of our being
the very centre of the heart.

Thinking, just how far we've come
and all the love we have
to give.

'Til Shiloh we chant.
(with apologies to Buju Banton)

I'm in the garden with my retired mother,
after deserting reality for some lack of respect.
Lunch done, equal orders. I stop amongst
the camping patioed bonsai to reflect at my action,
correct. Wonder at racism some dark motivation
before a knock at the front door.
A bearded casual foot soldier, in blue
dressed in tweed, before a foot and mouth joke
about fascism, some poor bullock in tweed
tamed by a trusting home-cooked wife.

He inveigles his way across the doorstep
in brogues, campaigning, to find the fitted carpet worn,
by admiring a diarama war scene, inanimate theatre-story
kept like best china in a glassless cabinet.
Is it Waterloo? The prospective politician asks
having some interest from the battles
he once fought at the front, in fatigues not tweed.

You must ask my brother I say, blood boiling
under a calm and inviting hospitable exterior
a thousand words mixed in my epidrome
stammered to pronounce.
We bandy words like democracy
to prove ourselves both free before
asking him to leave my birth-house.
And the cross on the paper he says with his eyes?

Talk talk of Kaliyuga would be masturbation here.
I hear now and then he joined the war cabinet
and advises for and against an appropriate carte blanche
bomb.

Peter Handley

The View from my friend The Drunk.

Trains ache into the station and out like puss.
Cars shoot across the over carriage that cuts the city in two,
screaming out of the urban solitude.
Last night's hue of neon aquamarine from the cinema complex,
as an environmental compliance please turn off unwanted lights,
now set to timer, the summer nights are here. I wonder.
From this apartment, stench of acrid cider and flatulence
leaving through the open windows, bleach and detergent.

We do have a choice. The view from here tells me so.
A green level playing field, the cemetery beyond,
overbearing, overgrown and overpopulated.
Clouds turn this new season with rapidity, from verdancy
to autumn in the whisp of a wind, Chernobyl anniversaries
Sunday roasts. Family meals. Protect and survive.
Adapt and survive. Skirmishes around turmoil passing as society
locked into radio stations, the new generation eating more sugar.

Here I am, that neo, neo. Not a word to waste
nor one to write that has not been written.
Adding to the coagulation of explanations and theories
that hurtle us beyond a millennium. To soothe and coerce.
Agitate and attend.
A little mirror that reflects just a little of that self loathing,
as we throw ourselves into the next new experience
brought to you by the everrevellingalwaysextollingnevercapitulating
landlords of excess.
In cafes we talk of children in classrooms we cannot control.

In the fruitmarket just in front of the life assurance buildings,
so it seems, in the city view. Bananas arrive
from another struggling republic.
A car boot sale in the yard with fruit and the detritus collecting
to form again in another attic for another year, or sell,
for the electricity bill or petrol tank or dividend for the man

in the life assurance building, ticking behind the fruitmarket.
An assured life will demonstrate the brilliance of living.
How you will feel the wind in your hair, the sand between your toes
because you know, you know, because the papers and the policies
tell you so, beyond the drain and drizel of second hand living.
A policy is a policy after all.

What would happen if construction stopped.
That there was no smoke and nor no fire.
A man walks into the shadow of his own virtual morality
and never comes back…
A woman takes the baby out of the bath water and a thirst
comes over her.
The after birth lies pungent in a jar in the corner.
The moon rips a tide across all the heavens.

In the park, sunshine high, two stories sit and talk.
Sometimes with each other. Sometimes across each other.
Both are wrapped in a mutuality that stings like an empty bottle
to some. They are getting there. Like mono rails,
they are getting there. They have been there before.
The relish of returning is what spurs them on. Spurring,
spurring as they do, the spurn and rejection of most others
is what takes them to it.

And the view from here is lovely. It really is nice.
It is beautiful just for an instant. Holding that instant
is the way to travel, the way to where they have been
before. Comfort in travelling all the way there
all that distance to arrive at the departure point.
Two stories telling tales.

A man tends a lawn on a gravestone bed.
Changes the water underneath a headstone and swims in a memory.
Dead daffodil heads. He cannot appreciate the two tales above him,
but then he has his memories. He *can* feel like crying but not today.
Today his tears are as locked as two tales talking on a bench,

about how they arrived, how they depart, how they get there,
how they'll get back.

What happens in the compromise of the original conviction ?
In the event, at the last count, the revolution come full circle,
the cycle of things.
Those same irascible desires and unfumigated psychological complaints
re-emerging now in the dim light of more experience, sifted,
segregated, made complicated by others' experience.
Are these words and have they come to complicate the uncomplicated.
Moving on. One step beyond the step we make for ourselves.
You stop the clock, to slow down time, to catch a thought, an image
or a notion, to ease your own living, find your own time.

I believe his technique relies on the fact that we are all, all,
aqueous broths of saltwater and ionic conductivity
and he is waiting for his moon.

Memory.

I remember, once upon a time, that was,
yes, that's it, I remember.
How once someone telling me
(and I can't for the life of me)
they, he, I'm sure he, telling me
that, now what was it, god, yes,
but it wasn't him, that deity thing,
he said, that's it now, god, yes
no one remembers, remembers
anything that isn't memorable.
That's like a sensation, like realising
the wetness in drink.
I remember, you don't remember
anything that isn't memorable.
He said to me, long ago now, it was,
he said no one remembers anything
that isn't memorable.

Serotonin re-uptake inhibitor.

I talk about the mystery of things
like I am God's spy to myself
like there is no one else, because there's not.
Beer. Book. Fag.
Besides these mobile calls that tell me
of stasis and depression, of pills
and paintings waiting, a brother and a lover
both turn their time to me, like synchronised
alarm clocks in my psyche, how I might
be wanted to dull their pain of loneliness.
And for me? Dharma. Immutable laws.
Stuck between a place that is neither
a house nor a home. I am legitimately
vagabond, accepted as the norm.

Living in this mystery of things
waiting to sign the contract with god,
currently being drawn up, I know
how it goes.

I try reason for myself. Rug pulled from
under of a sudden after four months
of sharing stories on the road.
Like a contracted marriage for children
we kill at the end.
Death. Loss. Loneliness.

The normal positive response
to depressive lovers, artistic brothers
leaves me cold, empty,
wanting to bark my own complaints
into this shithole world.
Serotonin.

Second Sunday in Advent.

I am in the pew, reading in a cathedral
somewhere in the west of England
where old kings fought old battles
for school children to memorise.

The reflection of burning prayer candles
in the shiny brass plaques
remind me of roaring home fires
of red, orange december days.

I light a prayer for my brother
to help him see himself, help
for himself. Retire to a chair
in the empty aisle
to read a little in contemplation
a book full of black poets,
though the odd Indian also pops in.
Skin.

The lady who comes to remove
the dead plastic candle cases
from the prayer racks
has little regard for peace
She throws them into a box
the din. For the final punch
in my solace, the loose change
echoes around the stone pillars
holding up religion as I learn
how not to sing in a Nigerian prison.

Peter Handley

Same as.

my brother says he's had it
if God doesn't throw him a line
while foreign inspectors in warmer climes
are shaking out their pockets
and fishermen are complaining
that their lines have been cut
by an oversized state bureaucracy,
that the seas are empty of their burdened concern.
my brother says he's had it.

For safety's sake

Which I've never understood
as safe is safe and needs no sake
a thing of beauty is best ignored
without explanation or recourse to nature.
Exponentially it'll eat you up
believe me, coming from a hermit
you'll be understanding a little why.

Blue telephone, red line
in a middle distance,
beckoning a move to resolution.
Give in to that
and you'll succumb to the devil
my mother used to say.
If she didn't she would've
had she not been predicated to housework.

It's shit, shit, all of it shit
he would say, with fervour and tea.
I would nod my head in assistance
to his behaviour. Mostly I knew though
that its shit was his.
I just wallowed in it pretending to be
happy as.

Treatment for the Whole Family.

Yesterday a hospital visit, a small
emergency for the pharmaceutically addicted
state-sponsored satiety for the artistically
inclined, another clandestine lie between
an ignorant Hippocrates and his blushing oath.

A hospital visit today, rushed like lightning
from this side of a country to the next
centre of excellence to excellence
to do something osteoporosis wise
and be the taxi healer still.

Another car ambulant to an appointment
may it never stop, this curse, as we live
to die. And die dead it does this one.
Remember how she said the small pink jar
held the remnants so courteously, that
she should call tomorrow to hear confidentially
how it might never have been born.

and tomorrow ?
My petri dish to the future
will reveal how it came to pass.

Colour.

Every conceivable thing I've done I've done
because it was conceived. Hmm.
It was the time of conception that's important
because that gave me the inception, impetus.

There are ten million colours in the universe
and they're just the ones we know.
We see.

But, because, and when, who's counting then.
The rain is blue tonight, underneath streetlights
yet the governing resource is green.

The hem of god's coat hangs down
never in the night, not even through defraction.
Mood, mood, but, but, because.

There is another colour, like not repugnant.
I see the hue around your head.
Things revealed I have conceived to you.
They were then, behind the time and
further off, now also, the distance
and the prescence of the end of the future.

Back in Blighty.

Six months, two love affairs, a kiss and colitis later
I may land up here at the back end o' nowhere
sipping hops and notating sentimental reflections

home, farm talk, tax talk and fast cars
no sea, no sewer, no indians and me the niggard.

November was a wicked month, it blew and rained
and ran the nose such fever foul upon a brow.
I'd shared soirees with teachers in their total belitterance
and my disbelief that such things exist, still, not a colony more a ghetto.
Talked fish with fattened fisherfolk mending nets with nylon thread
seen friends battered and bruised from fists and false promises.
 Laughed with the judges' son, poured money on the rich
chewed the cud that remains on the Ashram Gate.
Swapping jewellery with my diseased street girl
meant I also coiffured her kids, packed rice in bloated bellies.
In a short talk with a pissed up friend I discover the element
he says you're not like them I think I see,
You see you even think like us. Who could view it as a cliché?
You really fucked up this time. I did? Who sleeps?
The Us and Them Brigade begin again.

Chicken Seed.

In a town theatre that spawned the woman
who nearly killed culture
changing a political world, Grantham.
With screeching chocolate choked kids I sit
in red uniforms on red velvet seats.
I watch skeletons dance in the dark
the black light of ultra violet, a dancing dog.
At home, at sea, with an equally dark
black light doctor, fixing the dog.
The real story of the day
In white light, daylight, the order of the day.

C.21st Garden.again.

A bee is fooled by plastic foliage
how nature has been subsumed by man's folly.

In the village it takes two days
for brandy to water thin in the blood
and twenty seconds to enter the pin
on a mobile phone gone awry.
Grief takes two days as well I notice.
We have negotiated our vulnerabilities
re-invented the wheel for the race
proved peace abounds on the inside.
the bee agrees.

Things die, things are dead
a new life is in the offing, upping.
Something has begun.

A Secretary

comes into my sleeping room,
I'm not, but the room is, and begins
to take my quiet notes for tomorrow.
To clarify the projected days' activities
I reflect on the day past
the one I'm sleeping on, or not, but the room.
It came and went and is going in shorthand
a kind of compromise for the sake of time
it being an underhand and overborne perception.
It's turning in today, says the secretary.
I agree and say, you're right it is.

Tomorrow a secretary will come into
my sleeping room and on finding a tired
and flacid eejit
couched in white
with burning wings put on the windowsill
will tear out yesterday's page
and project a novel into the face of a
dieing angel.
Angels come and go.

Only a thought

I hold the sun in my left hand
as I cross the border to you
immigration centres are being established
for American refugees coming to Africa;
they get it, all over again
home to love, if they could.

Driving East. A Christmas Morning.

I saw the sun-rise over Cambridge-east
that cold crisp christmas morning. Stopped
dead in my tracks flying from home to home
to yet more love. Blinded by that orange shimmering ball
against the blue of a dawn, just before the night
lights went out on an arterial island road.

Two planes' whispers in the ether kiss and cross
in mid-air leaving their vapours
to gossip of an affair spent passing mid atlantic.

Further on down the road a curse
at the counter Shell Girl working against her will
on this day, early (as kids have already unwrapped gifts)
laughing with a George or a Bert about how bright
the day and miserable the staff. Coffee, caffeine.
Grim on this day George.

On, screeching hard out of a station of negativity
watching an earth glory rise high, higher.
At the county border sign a stop again to praise
an orange glow. Home, where it is
and how we go there, lightfooted to and fro
beneath the winter sun.

Christmas Day News.

Birth of hope, sign of peace, opposition to war unjust.

Israeli forces pull back from Manger Square in Bethlehem.
No decorations and no sign of X-Mas.

Pray for peace says the Catholic Cardinal.

A water pipe bursts in Scotland and three ticket holders
win the Lotto jackpot.

Showers over Wales and south east England

and that is the news at three minutes past five.

Every December sky, I dream of the spring.

Only one way. Text.

In the graveyard communing with a fox.

Moonbathing on a cold thames beach
are you still shmeeting in t'orifice.

Not angry with you, but the world
but the world and her uncle.

mid-winter. Ockendon.

Oak leaves on the ground outside the door
on the estate, the estate we're in.
What does it say, mean, being here
at the beginning, the end, wi' the scag 'eads
and the white multifarious van man.

A pattern is emerging, a pattern it makes on t'ground
you know the pattern it makes Robin Hood.
Around the Major Oak in a minor key you make.

Social junglist Friday neet politricks they think
like they're knowing, bling bling. Music.
Fuck fick jingle jungle jangle, the oak.
My teeth grind sitting on me ass, 'ickle rass.
There are oak leaves outside the door.

Secretary General – Women's League.

The beauty of the woman that knows
is
that it is.
Not displayed and the opposite
it sits, she sits
just behind herself and vulnerability
knowing it, knowing the coming
doing it anyway, for the doing
having the power and giving it away.

Late Utility Upkeep.

'invention is the way the mind seizes upon an inconspicuous occurrence'.

The shelf sat above the electric cooking range
tidily painted into its yellow corner
in the food preparation room of a
small rented apartment on the estate.

It was retrieved from a neighbour's garbage bin
slats of cheap Norwegian pine going to the dump,
sat next to our own for a while
waiting for a lick of paint
and the measured appraisal of the trainee
do it yourself man; screws and plugs
in a brown paper hardware sachet
sitting in wait in the bits of everything drawer.

The usual suspect shelf putter upper
has made his inspection and declared it fit
for his daughter's kitchen
leaving his question mark like why
the span of its tongue has not touched both walls.

When I am gone, so goes the shelf and my apprenticeship.
Tomorrow, there will be another range, another inspection
Shall I be there to explain the invention
And it's purpose.

The Bench.

A solid lump of dog shit
(vegetarian dog I notice)
wrapped and tied in a freezer bag
left unattended on the end of a bench
at a bend in the river
reminds me, I could be here,
I could be there, any fuckin' where
in this Great Britain Plc.

On Westminster Bridge – a postcard for Sunil.
(with no apology to Bill Wordsworth, poet)

an Omnibus crosses the bridge
of ambivalent nostalgia, towards truth
against the backdrop of mother democracy
airing her dirty washing like flags
in the wind, imperial measurement.

a happy nuclear family crossing east
half past the hour of midday
chased by common man, head down
in a hard hat, going home from graft.
It is coming those naked resilient truths
out of the house of lords and lately ladies
Blows east and east to west
the shipping forecast
above old father thames
his addled and toxic fish
trying to find the sea
a tirade route home free
in a shoal of their own making.
Half past the hour of midnight,
towards dawn, a white and slightly soiled
dove above the palaces of power
is cooing in solitude.

Not John Wonnacott.

My brother's inability to come to terms
with his self leaves me distraught.
Often it goes something like

I haven't got a partner
I can't love myself enough
I haven't got a full time job
There isn't a place I belong

It is more than a modern malaise
it is a dis-ease of the heart
heart and mind malady.

I try, he tries, we try, are very trying
to slowly turn the world upside down
from here, and there, occasionally win
but it's hard brother, it is hard.

I can have the things I want
out of my life, the I, the I, the I.
It would be such a waste
if
I died as I have much to offer
more to fulfil.

When the only thing that makes
you happy, is making yourself miserable
do one thing brother

Start tomorrow and ask ten people
what security is
it's not a man with a shotgun
outside an ATM in New California
it's not, it's not, it's not.
Change the image, give it out

offer daffodils to a deity
kiss the stars with your arse.

Noah's New Boat.

I hear the sound of the drums
from far off places beating
awareness into this town
of misbegots, my town
Salute the progress in my absence
and savour it like a king.

The old ballet teacher
hides her head in shame
recovering what she lost.

At the end of the age of innocence
when the directive to dream
became apparent
I noticed, in that finite ward
that is my birthplace
an attitude that began to become
the beginning of understanding
spreading steadily amongst it all
that there is living hope
in this new ark
and me gone somewhere else.

Night shift sister. Casualty Dept.

1.32am
How do you feel about yourself.
Why
Sure
Sure
How much counselling and help have you had
What sort of counselling
When did you last see her
Sure
Take your time

…hmm

did she teach you techniques
not always so easy eh ?

2.13am
…hmm

no
scratch my head red raw
slow down
big deep breathing

hmm…
hmm…

sure.

3.17am
hmm…

right
how were you when you were there

hmm…
hmm…

do you enjoy it
it's always a worry
if it's the right thing for your life.

4.22am
doesn't mean
pathway… bollocks
what did you teach
Ok you didn't
Does that mean there are no more offers

hmm…

5.01am
How long ago did that relationship finish
Quite a while

hmm…hmm

no shame in that
why
so you don't like yourself very much at the moment
how long have you been feeling like that for

no

so do you socialise with people now
all the things you wish you had.

5.49am
does that make you feel worse
so you don't help each other
how many brothers
what about mum, how do you get on with her

how long have you been staying in…

a doctor comes. 6.12am. A psychiatrist comes.

A doctor comes again. 6.41am.

A nurse comes. The doctor comes again.

Prescription.

By 7am we have the medication and are on our way home.

The Little Klowne.

directives are coming from another place
to paint the fool into the race
and far from here, upon a hill
(after a certain period of growing up
a ripening of wisdom, toilet training
homelessness and hopeless enterprise
learning, teaching and more growing up)
a pen is lifted to a fathers' address
never complete it seems because of death.

History Lesson.

What is the little clown doing now
I wonder, I wonder.
What is the little clown doing now
She wears a new dress
I wonder I wonder
She wears a new dress
like a frown.
Where will the clown go to now
I wonder I wonder
Where will the clown go to now
She'll travel the world
in the new dress I bought
and the frown in the gown
will go down.

Literare rey Hovel.London.

Just arrived, kicking and screaming, ranting double dutch
t' the oxford educator, ferdee, ferdah, rah, rah, rah.
Walk shy of the parable, smelt it melt it before and shall
again. So.
As the social welfare officer for the barkers of Barnby
for the day, missed the lift. Happen upon
the soup of the day Jimmy Burns
just fer the People's Passion in the Whiskey cafe.
So much Blooms bury, so much as Mr McCabe
stares behind me, into a book I presume
Someone else in black and white has farewelled to Mayo
and I can tell yer, he been there, and back
in walks the lift, surreptitiously, serendipity.

They are my care assistants and me theirs.
It begins all over again.
I am in the driving seat.

Dryad. unfinished this.

Mrs Clarke was lost somewhere in memory,
that place between then and now
where we can go to when we find ourselves confused
by existence. It wasn't an unhappiness.
It wasn't a vague feeling of unknowing,
but I could see, in the way she sat and played
with the band of gold on her index finger
that she was thinking about her lover
and about her abandoned infidelity.

During the final months of my pregnancy
I had occasion often to visit the botanical gardens
and sit with Mrs. Clarke. It was as if my unborn
first daughter was drawing strength from the beech tree.
If thoughts transmute through an unconscious
morphic resonance between persons
then why not all living things
and what greater prescence to be under, in awe of,
than this sprawling beech
and all it's inherent age and wisdom.

No money in poetry.

The publisher, manager of fine words on paper
bound between graphically designed cardboard
covers, is giving a list of indigenous poets,
for my reading, reference, education and
intellectual cultural support. It is a given
and received.

In a bookshop later, two slim volumes
of fine words on paper bound between
graphically designed cardboard covers, symbols
and intimations of the words that lie between.

He is furnished, or decorated with some of mine
favourite purveyors of purple prose in common
language, find examples of such on bookshelves
for sale. 'Good, but I shan't buy it' he says 'simply
find what I want on the web'.
I wish him every success in all the tomes he stands
or sits to rich from. Printing books, editing words
and putting them out onto bookshelves .

P : poetry
art for our sake.

There was only one person in the audience
It was all for them
We didn't know, in the light,
 if it was a man or a woman,
 We never found out.
They applauded and left

It was the best show we'd done in ages
we all agreed.

(From Hurt's Dictum)

Printed in Great Britain
by Amazon